Playing your own golf game is a participative guide
designed to enable you and your coach to realise your true
potential. It's not the usual detailed A–Z golf instruction
manual. This book sets out key fundamentals, evaluates
your current game, and tailors an improvement plan where
your game needs it most. Your journey of discovery is
about to begin.

STRIKING THE WHITE PUBLICATIONS S W

Playing your own golf game

For anyone who wants to build their own great golf game

Rohan Dummett and Tim Pembroke

The team

Concept and development: Timothy Pembroke – Pembroke Development Corporation
Golf technical direction: Rohan Dummett – Rohan Dummett Golf Instruction
Golf model: Jason Day – World and Australian Junior Golf Champion 2004
Physiotherapist: Ramsay McMaster – Melbourne Golf Injury Clinic
Colour and Style: Hayesberrytehan
Graphic design: Andrew Cunningham – Studio Pazzo
Photographer: Gerrard Warrener – Digital Photography Inhouse
Illustrator: Mark McKaige – HSJ Advertising
Editor: Margaret Trudgeon
Production support: Sarah Crichton

Striking the White Publications
www.playingyourowngolfgame.com.au

First published 2005

National Library of Australia
Cataloguing-in-Publication data:

Dummett, Rohan, 1963– .
Playing your own golf game: for anyone who wants to build their own great golf game.

ISBN 0 646 44092 6.

1. Golf. I. Pembroke, Timothy, 1960– . II. Title.

796.352

Printed and bound in China by Everbest Printing

Readers are advised to seek professional medical advice before undertaking any of the exercises and drills presented in this book. The author, publisher and every other person and company involved in the publication, distribution and sale of the book shall not accept responsibility for any injury or claim arising directly or indirectly from the information contained in this book.

Dedication

This book is dedicated to all my fellow golf coaches, both past and present, who have dedicated their careers to helping others enjoy the great game of golf.

Rohan Dummett

Acknowledgements

Thanks to the following coaches who all enthusiastically and professionally worked on improving my game.

Australia: Alan Bull, Rohan Dummett, Charlie Earp, Richard Hatt,
Ross Herbert, Peter Heiniger, Alex Mercer, David Merriman, Laurie Montague,
Denis McDade and Randel Vines
England: Peter Ballingall, Leslie King, Steven Gould, David Wilkinson, and David Talbot

Tim Pembroke

Author's note

While the illustrations in this book feature a right-handed male golfer, the fundamentals are the same for both left-handed and female golfers.

This book has been designed to be used by the golfer with their coach. In general, the level of technical detail is elementary. Your coach will provide additional technical instruction as your game requires it.

Foreword

I started playing golf at the age of five. My initial teacher was my grandfather, who lived at the back of Sunshine Park in Melbourne, and we hit balls onto the football ovals. My golf heroes were Jack Nicklaus and Tom Watson, and I remember poring over famous books like Jack Nicklaus's *Golf My Way* in an effort to improve my own fundamentals.

As good as these books were, their influence was only minor in comparison to Bruce Green, my first and most influential coach. When I was 13 Bruce encouraged me and told me I could be whatever I wanted to be. I then moved to Perth at age 17 and came under the tutorage of Ross Metherell at Collier Park. Through a combination of participating in junior golf programs and a lot of hard work and determination, I was gradually able to realise my dream of becoming a successful golf professional.

What I like most about **Playing your own golf game** is the recognition that developing your skills without a coach is all but impossible, and that you and your coach need to work to a targeted plan and not just randomly continue with haphazard lessons. Hours and hours of well-intentioned practice will not guarantee results. In order to improve, it is essential that you and your coach carry out an evaluation of your current game, and then set specific goals with a regular plan to achieve those goals.

Like any sport, starting young is ideal, which is why I spend considerable time promoting The Schweppes Junior Golf clinics run by local professionals. Those juniors that show promise have the opportunity to participate in golf foundations like The Jack Newton Junior Golf Foundation in NSW and Graham Marsh Junior Golf in WA. Beyond that, state and national programs are the pinnacle of amateur golf. These excellent programs are why Australia has competed, and will continue to compete, well above its weight division throughout the world.

For those golfers who miss out on these programs, **Playing your own golf game** is an inspired new initiative which should dramatically improve the way the 'weekend golfer' is taught. Too often, older golfers continue to pursue technical excellence at the expense of short game and course management practice. Learn to accept your natural swing and work within it.

I have always been a fader of the ball and have learnt to manage my golf game no matter what the course set-up. Johnny Miller once paid me and all weekend golfers the ultimate compliment of saying that 'I swung it like a 15 handicapper'! That week his comment inspired me to win the Ford Open on the US Tour by holing a 6 iron on the first play-off hole. While you may not have the opportunity to play the PGA Tour and win a tournament, your own swing could take you to great success and enjoyment.

I strongly commend this book to golfers of all ages and abilities seeking to improve their game. Who knows – maybe a few more will be joining the ever-growing list of Australian professional golfers on the world tours.

Enjoy!

Craig Parry
Sydney, Australia

Contents

Introduction

Playing your own golf game is the brainchild of Tim Pembroke and Rohan Dummett. I first met Tim in London in 1990 when I was playing on the European tour. He was and remains an enthusiastic lover of golf, who over the years has worked hard at his game to progress from a beginner to maintaining a single figure handicap.

I first met and played tournaments with Rohan in 1985. He has developed into one of Australia's leading PGA golf coaches, looking after a number of touring professionals. He also teaches weekend golfers at his golf school in Albert Park, Melbourne, where he and his PGA-qualified staff give over 12,000 lessons a year.

Looking back over his own learning journey, Tim realised that the weekend golfer was not benefiting from the more structured and holistic methods being used in junior and elite amateur programs. He presented his dilemma as a challenge to Rohan, and together they have created a solution with **Playing your own golf game**. They believe that if keen weekend golfers divert their time away from searching for technical perfection to working with a coach on a balanced improvement plan, they would be far happier and less frustrated golfers.

The first part of the book lays the framework and fundamentals to be applied in the 'Make your practice count' section. It's a clever mix of old and new ideas, presented with traditional Anthony Ravielli style, detailed illustrations in a modern colour scheme. The book's only quote comes from the great man, Jack Nicklaus. It powerfully illustrates how arguably the strongest mind ever to play golf put himself 'in the zone'.

Playing your own golf game is a bold, inspired challenge to both players and coaches to change the way they learn and teach. It is revolutionary in providing a universal framework for golf coaches to evaluate and plan a player's lesson and practice program of improvement. The player's journey is documented with lesson notes and drills to remind them what matters most in improving their game.

If you need some guidance with your golf, then taking the journey with **Playing your own golf game** is a guaranteed winner.

Happy golfing.

Brett Ogle
Sydney, Australia

1
Frustrations of the game

Ever been tempted to give up golf in total frustration because your game doesn't seem to be improving? Despite hours of practice and numerous lessons, you just haven't been able to lower your handicap or score. It has plateaued at the same level for years. The essence of this book is to provide you with a guide to the galaxy of golf. And believe us, it is a galaxy – full of myths, self-help books, videos, DVDs, CD-ROMs and your own generally incorrect assessment of your abilities and misconceptions about the game.

This book aims to improve your game by providing you with a unique, interactive guide for you and your coach. While reinforcing the technical aspects of golf, you can record your personal journey as you master the fundamentals and improve your game.

Lost in space

Golf is a game where hours of well-intended practice can cause more harm than good. The professional golfer makes the game look deceptively easy with his or her apparently natural swing. Golf is, in fact, a far more natural game than most people realise. **The problem is that the majority of golfers develop poor swing mechanics as a result of receiving poor information.**

Most of us were taught our bad habits when we began playing golf. We labour along with those habits for years, often not even realising the limiting effect our poor technique is having on our game.

You may find that when your golf swing is eventually corrected by your coach it will feel awkward and contrived for a while.

The ideal scenario is to work with a coach before you develop any such poor habits, so that your natural ability is enhanced by correct information and good coaching early on in your golfing career.

THE IMPORTANCE OF GOAL SETTING

Both authors of this book have experienced and observed many people give up golf in frustration because of a lack of reward for all their endeavours. To avoid this, you need to remain motivated and focused.

What you need is a golf plan. This is where you write down the goals you want to achieve and how you balance your practice and game time to achieve them. It's not dissimilar to the way a business owner forms a business plan. You'd be surprised at the number of high-achieving community leaders and professionals who spend the vast majority of their week building and implementing strategies for their business, while they are quite content to approach their golf game in a completely disorganised and haphazard manner.

Making a golf plan is explained in Chapter 4. Before this plan can be established you need first to engage a coach (Chapter 2) and have him or her make a detailed evaluation of your whole game (Chapter 3).

It's important to set goals that are measurable. Goals that are handicap or score-driven are usually best. Golf is a game where both amateur and professional golfers are judged by score. Therefore the goal of this book is ultimately to assist you in lowering your score.

If you are a golf range junkie who just loves to smack the ball with your driver as far as you can into the distance, this book is guaranteed to disappoint you. Improving your game through practice is about more than just hitting balls at the driving range hour after hour.

Putting, for example, accounts for roughly 40 per cent of a golfer's total score. How many golfers spend 40 per cent of their time practising putting on the practice green? It's easy to get lost in chasing the adrenalin rush of smashing the driver in preference to practising those short putts.

By setting your goal to 'lower your score', you need to take a holistic approach to practice and lessons with your coach. Working on your fitness, golf course management and understanding the psychology of golf are all key elements to lowering your score.

The problem is that the majority of golfers develop poor swing mechanics as a result of receiving poor information.

The benefits of a coach

You may have tried to improve your game through the use of self-help books, videos and magazines. The problem with such material is that it isn't geared to your personal situation. Are you built like Tiger Woods and have been learning the game since the age of three, or are you middle-aged, unfit and just beginning to play? Your age, your physical condition and your experience of golf all affect how you should attempt to swing a golf club.

This is where the assistance of a golf coach becomes essential in preference to the 'do it yourself' philosophy. **All great players, like Tiger Woods, Greg Norman and Jack Nicklaus, have or had their own coach who knows every aspect of their game, including their strengths and weaknesses.** They know how to steer their player through the game so that they can play it to their optimum ability. It's almost impossible to improve your game without expert guidance and tuition.

Take a moment to flick through the pages of this book. Notice the number of work pages in Chapter 7. These pages are designed for you and your coach to evaluate your current game, set an improvement plan and make notes relating to your progress. You can write down the drills your coach has prescribed, document your successes and failures, and list your practice notes. Many lessons have gone to waste when a week later the player can't accurately remember the contents of the lesson, causing them to inaccurately perform prescribed drills. By noting things down, you can effectively retain and use the information you have been given in your golf lessons.

The great news is that your copy of this book will record your personal progress via evaluation charts, statistics and notes.

This may seem like a significant investment of time and money but remember that, unlike many other sports, golf is a game for a lifetime and your investment now will ensure an effective and efficient structure to realising your full potential for this wonderful game. Without it you may remain forever 'lost in space'.

All great players have or had their own coach who knows every aspect of their game, including their strengths and weaknesses.

Fleeting success

Have you ever been on the range hitting the ball particularly well one day, and then come back the very next day with enormous anticipation, only to find the magic has disappeared? On the first day a series of swing-thoughts and movements consistently produced near-perfect shots. It all felt so easy and rhythmic. The ball felt sweet off the club face. It felt like you had all the time in the world to get the club from the top of the backswing back to the ball. Shot after shot sailed long and straight. It felt automatic. You were enjoying things so much that you hit 200 balls and didn't want to go home.

The next day, however, was a totally different story. Nothing went right. You couldn't quite find the middle of the club face. You felt jerky and quick. The previous day's swing-thoughts and movements didn't seem to work any more. Something had changed. What had happened?

When things were going well you had found a series of moves that were effective for you, and a rhythm and timing to put it all into a sequence that also worked. **For many average golfers, the golf swing is a complicated series of movements made inconsistent through compensatory adjustments with each and every swing.**

When the sequence of movements, together with timing and rhythm, are accurately adjusted the results can be great. Because such co-ordination requires intricate precision, what appears to be a sound and efficient swing can fall apart in the blink of an eye.

When the ball striking was consistently great, each swing came from the short-term memory. In other words, you had a feel for every tiny adjustment and movement required to produce a swing good enough to hit a nice solid shot. It seemed easy because the feeling was so fresh in your mind that repeating this action over and over was a relatively simple task.

Because we all love to practise the things we are good at, it seemed logical to keep going, hitting more and more balls in an attempt to ingrain those movements so they became automatic. Unfortunately, once you had found your winning formula almost all those practice balls hit thereafter were a waste of time. This may sound a little harsh, but the proof was evident when you returned to the range the very next day only to find the magic had disappeared. Running off your short-term memory can give you a false sense of security.

Take this mathematical equation, for example. What is 120 divided by 6? The answer is, of course, 20. How long did it take you to come up with the answer? One, maybe two seconds? Now read the same mathematical question again. What is 120 divided by 6? The answer, of course, is 20. How long did it take you to come up with the answer this time? Only a split second, I am sure.

The same applies to a golf swing. When you get to the range, you warm up and start searching for a series of movements to produce well-struck, accurate shots. After a while you find this co-ordination. Once you have it, repeating it is easy because the time taken between shots is minimal, so the sensation of the swing stays in the front of the conscious mind, or the short-term memory. **However, the best type of practice is to search, find, rest and repeat the process**. In other words, when you are at the range working on your golf swing and you feel like you have achieved your goal or found your winning formula, instead of continuing to belt balls, stop, walk away, practise a different facet of your game, such as chipping or putting, or simply have a break before going back to search and find your winning formula again.

The more often you search and find, the less the find time becomes, until eventually there is no find time at all. This is where the great players are at. They can walk onto the range after a stretch and hit some beautifully struck shots first up. They don't have to hit 50 balls to find a series of movements that work for them.

To play consistently good golf you need to reach this level. It can only be achieved by effective practice to a carefully laid-out plan. **What good is reeling off 200 balls on the range in an hour or so when in an hour on the golf course a typical 100-shooter will only hit around 10 to 15 full shots**.

In Chapter 4 we establish your golf calendar and divide it into what we describe as red and green zones, red indicating the time when you are building your game, and green representing the time when you concentrate on playing your game. We then create your time wheel as it relates to the five key areas of the game – golf plan, technical, physical, mental and playing. In order for coaches to devise your golf plan, they first need to conduct a thorough analysis of your overall game. This is carried out in Chapter 3, 'History tells a story'.

2

Choosing a coach

Choosing a coach is without doubt the most important golfing decision you will have to make. The expert guidance and tuition of a coach is the only truly effective way that you will reach your desired goal of lowering your score.

You can find a coach by enquiring at your favourite golf course, golf club or driving range. There are also listings on the internet and in the phone book. Golf coaches are like any professional and vary in skill, price, accessibility and enthusiasm. We have provided a few pointers to help you make your selection.

How to make the right choice

Take your time about choosing your coach. Once you've made your choice, listen to your coach and your coach only. No one else. If I need my car fixed, I go to a mechanic. If I need a house built, I consult an architect and a builder. If I am ill, I consult a doctor. It therefore makes no sense that so many golfers seem prepared to take advice from almost anyone around them. These are usually well-meaning golfing buddies who have read the latest golf magazine tips and think you might benefit from them. Forget it. Ninety-nine per cent of the time these seemingly helpful tips will not apply to your game and may well have been misinterpreted by your friend.

It's possible that you may have at least one lesson with several different coaches before you feel able to choose one with confidence. Having chosen one, stick with that coach for at least one year.

WHAT DOES A COACH DO?

Coaches are there to help you improve your game and therefore your enjoyment of the game. They will begin by evaluating your current abilities (as set out in Chapter 3) and go on to plan an effective lesson program for you, prescribing drills to help you work on any weak areas. These can be recorded in this book, along with any practice notes, so that you can monitor your progress along the way.

MAKING THE INVESTMENT

Playing your own golf game provides a teaching framework that will only be successful if both player and coach commit to a planned series of lessons over a period of at least one year. We suggest you discuss paying in advance and, in return, your coach should be able to offer some form of discount.

Making the big decision

Consider the following factors when deciding which coach to work with. These helpful tips will help you make the 'right' choice.

ACCESSIBILITY
- World-renowned coaches might be great, but can you get an appointment to see them? They must be available on an ongoing basis.

PROXIMITY
- Golf is time-consuming enough without spending two hours travelling to a lesson. If you can't see a coach because he or she is too far away geographically, look for a good coach who's closer to home.

PRACTICAL
- Make sure they don't overload you with too many swing-thoughts to practise at once. Having started with an overview, the best policy is to isolate and work on one specific area at a time rather than everything at once. It may mean repeating the same specific advice over several lessons until you get it right. A good coach has the confidence not to stray from a logical order of technical priorities.

PERSONALITY
- Qualities needed are enthusiasm, humour, good listening skills and empathy.

TECHNICAL
- Does your coach continue to learn the latest coaching methods? Do they use video/computer analysis where a picture can tell you a thousand words?

MENTOR
- Your coach should provide holistic guidance and a structured approach to learning. He or she should be keen to coach you in all areas of the game, not just full swing fundamentals. Expect your coach to help you set and evaluate goals and keep you motivated to succeed.

3

History tells a story

We believe that to teach golf effectively coaches first need to conduct a thorough evaluation of their player. This is not only to assess the player's golf swing, but to comprehensively understand beliefs and concepts the player might hold about the golf swing, their realtive state of physical fitness and well-being, and the golf equipment he or she uses.

A full analysis of your complete golf game

A full analysis of your golf game by your coach involves:

- **mental evaluation**
- **technical evaluation**
- **physical evaluation**
- **equipment evaluation**
- **taking statistics**

Once your coach has compiled information on the first four areas, he or she will be able to fully understand your particular strengths and weaknesses. This will allow your coach to set realistic goals and prepare your golf plan, with your player's calendar and golf time wheel (see Chapter 4, pages 40–44).

Before you do anything, you will need to answer a series of questions so your coach can understand some of your core beliefs relating to your golf technique. Your coach needs to understand exactly what you are thinking. Ideally, this is done either before your initial lesson or second lesson when you start to use **Playing your own golf game**. We also provide an on-course self-assessment to see how well you prepare and focus during a round of golf.

At your first lesson, your coach should also begin a technical assessment of the various aspects of your game. These include grip, set-up, alignment, club face, pivot, plane, radius and impact. It can be completed in its entirety during the first lesson or over the course of the first few lessons.

Your coach also needs to understand your physical condition before he or she can effectively work on your golf swing and fully understand the limitations you may face physically while swinging a club. A series of self-test drills appear on pages 144–149 of Chapter 7, which you should perform to evaluate your present physical condition.

Next, your equipment should be assessed. Having your equipment correctly fitted will make changing your swing easier as you won't have to compensate for golf clubs that don't suit you.

Finally, it's time to take some round statistics that will assist your coach to understand your strengths and weaknesses.

Compiling all this information may take a few lessons, but it will be time and money well spent as it will allow the coach to set you an effective golf plan and lesson program.

Mental evaluation – What are you thinking?

First of all, your coach needs to know exactly what you are thinking – that is, what you believe you should be doing when you swing a golf club. Your coach will then work on ridding you of any misconceptions relating to golf technique – no matter how small – that you may have. This is because you may be carrying a belief or concept around in your mind that is detrimental to your improvement. These include such common misconceptions or myths as 'keep your head still', 'keep your left arm straight' and 'tuck your trailing elbow in during the backswing'. These poor concepts will almost certainly cause severe swing problems; however, plenty of golfers have created their golf swings using these misconceptions as the cornerstone of their technique.

Tell the coach what you believe to be true. You may not necessarily be thinking of these concepts at a conscious level with every golf shot. Many of your core beliefs lie buried deep within the subconscious mind. You need to bring as many of these beliefs as you can to the surface for your coach. Unless they are out in the open for discussion, learning is all but impossible. If your coach is trying to help you implement a swing change, any belief you hold that is in opposition to the attempted change will render the change ineffective.

We have compiled a questionnaire for you to answer that will help to bring to the surface as many of your beliefs as possible. A sample is shown below, with the complete set of questions on pages 138–143 of Chapter 7. This is followed by an on-course self-assessment which will indicate whether your preparation and course management need work.

Sample – What are you thinking?   (circle and comment)

- Should your grip pressure be reasonably firm during the full swing?   **Yes /** (No)

  Held as lightly as possible.

To get the most out of this exercise we strongly urge you to complete the questionnaire on pages 138–143 before reading on.

Technical evaluation – Your current game

Your coach should grade every aspect of your game, from driving to putting, by filling out the technical evaluation charts on pages 128–130 of Chapter 7. A sample is provided below. Having done this, your coach can formulate a practice plan specific to your needs. The re-evaluation chart on pages 131–133 can be filled out when your coach considers reasonable progress has been made.

Sample – Coach's evaluation (✔ tick the standards)

Full swing						Date: 21/10/04		
	GRIP	SET-UP	ALIGN	CLUB FACE	PIVOT	PLANE	RADIUS	IMPACT
EXCELLENT								
WORKABLE							✔	
NEEDS WORK	✔	✔		✔	✔	✔		✔
POOR			✔					

COMMENTS

A grip that is quite weak, where the hands are rotated too far to the left, contributed to a set-up with no spine angle, resulting in open shoulders. To compensate you have a closed feet alignment and due to grip, an open club face throughout the swing. The result is a reverse pivot with an out to in swing plane through impact.

Physical evaluation – Getting fit for golf

Golf is a far more physical game than most people realise. The golf swing is an athletic movement and extremely taxing on the human body, largely because of the design of the golf club. The shaft can be up to 47 inches long. This, combined with the weight of the club head, means that the leverage required to swing the club places a huge strain on the body.

Research has shown that eight times your body weight goes through your lower back at impact. Many muscles throughout your body are activated in a good golf swing, with 90 per cent of your body working through it. No other sport puts such demands on the body.

At whatever level you play, the body's range of movement is challenged in many areas – strength, co-ordination, flexibility, balance and endurance.

Never before has so much attention and importance been placed on physical condition. Today's champion golfers are athletes who exercise to maximise their fitness. The average weekend golfer can also benefit enormously by keeping their body fit and balanced for golf.

A very high percentage of golfers can't swing the club effectively because their body isn't strong or flexible enough, or they have developed an imbalance through injury or one-sided dominance, sometimes due to playing other sports. These physical imbalances can prevent a player from adapting to technique changes.

Over a period of years most people's bodies tend to become a little stiff in the joints, resulting in loss of range of movement. Because of a lack of specific exercise, the muscles continually contract, so they become less flexible, leading to postural changes. This postural breakdown particularly affects people who sit at a desk or a computer all day. They often get hunched over, and this can have a significant negative effect on the golf swing.

There is a sample self-test on the next page. The complete set of five tests appears on pages 144–149 of Chapter 7. In the event that your coach considers that your physical condition needs further evaluation we have provided a postural screening survey to be completed by a physiotherapist on pages 150–151 of Chapter 7. This screening summary is designed for the physiotherapist who may not have extensive experience with the specific movements required in a golf swing.

Sample
Self-test 1 Extension drill – Angel wings against wall

Stand with your back against a wall. Pull your shoulder blades back and down towards your tailbone, tuck your chin in as though you are making a double chin, and suck your belly button in towards your spine. Place the backs of your arms, the backs of your hands and thumbs against the wall. Keep your feet together, pointing directly forwards, with the backs of your heels against the wall with your shoes on.

CHECK (CIRCLE YOUR ANSWER)	DATE: 15/9/04	DATE: 15/3/05
Shoulders against wall	(YES)/NO	(YES)/NO
Wrists against wall	YES/(NO)	(YES)/NO
Middle of back against wall	YES/(NO)	(YES)/NO
Skull against wall	(YES)/NO	(YES)/NO

Equipment evaluation – Equip yourself for the journey

A correctly fitted set of golf clubs rewards your best swing. This means that the club will allow you to make a smooth, balanced motion, free of compensatory moves that poorly fitted clubs will encourage.

Incorrectly fitted clubs help cause swing flaws as the golfer attempts to make up for the deficiencies of the club. The best players in the world are very particular about the equipment they use. Correctly fitted golf clubs are among the most underrated components of playing good golf.

If a golf club is too stiff in the shaft flex, for example, the golfer will usually labour with his or her swing. Poor timing and excessive hip and torso movement are common during the swing. Trying to hit the golf ball too hard is very common with overly stiff shafts because the shaft gives no assistance to the golfer. The correct flex facilitates a smooth swing, creating sufficient club head speed with less physical effort.

There seems to be an odd tendency for golfers to use shafts that are too stiff for them. It's almost a show of strength that if you use a stiff shaft it means you must be a good player. Don't be ashamed to use a softer shaft if you see some improved results.

If a golfer uses clubs that are too short, postural problems may occur, making an athletic golf swing very unlikely. This type of shaft length problem often results in off-centre contact with the ball and can cause a very low, weak ball flight. If a golfer is using a driver with too little loft, there is a tendency to sit on the back foot at impact and in the follow-through. This off-balance finish can cause lower back trouble due to arching of the spine, as the golfer attempts to get the ball airborne. A driver with the correct amount of loft on the club face will encourage a swing with less compensation and greater balance. These are just some examples, there are many more problems that can occur.

Using golf clubs that suit your golf game is vital if you wish to reach anywhere near your potential as a golfer. Just as no two people share the same fingerprint, no two people swing the golf club in exactly the same way. Standard golf clubs are only suitable for a small percentage of the golfing population, however, many people use them. If no two golfers have exactly the same swing characteristics, why are the majority of golfers in the world using golf clubs built to standard specifications?

When it comes to golf clubs there is a theoretical standard. The standards set are in shaft length, club head, lie angle, shaft flexibility and so on. This is fine. Standard is only the starting point, not the finishing point in club selection. Your golf clubs need to be tailored to suit you.

HOW DO I KNOW WHICH SPECIFICATIONS ARE RIGHT FOR ME?

The first step in selecting the correct golf equipment for yourself is to talk to your coach. He or she should be trained in the art of club-fitting or know someone who is. A good club-fitter's skills are not developed overnight. They are very much acquired skills. The ball flight, the sound of the club hitting the ball, the distance the ball travels, the effect the club has on your swing, how centred the hit is, and your view, are all very important to a good club-fitter. Teaching and fitting go hand in hand. We strongly believe that your coach is the best person to advise you in selecting your golf equipment.

On the opposite page is an example of a club evaluation chart. On pages 134–135 of Chapter 7 we provide a blank chart for you and your coach to fill out, together with a fitting chart should new clubs be required. Be prepared to pay for your coach's time during the fitting process. It will be money well spent.

If your coach is satisfied with your current set of clubs after having evaluated them, nothing more needs to be done in this area. At the very least, you will have newfound confidence in your equipment, knowing that you are not having to compensate for incorrect specifications. On the other hand, if your equipment proves to be less than satisfactory, it's worth talking to your coach about the possibility of purchasing something more suitable.

Using golf clubs that suit your golf game is vital if you wish to reach anywhere near your potential as a golfer.

DO YOUR CLUBS SUIT YOU?

Your coach will note down the specifications of your current clubs. If he or she considers them to be unsuitable, you will be recommended to have a club-fitting session. This could be done by your coach, or golf shop fitting expert.

Sample – Club evaluation chart – Do your clubs suit you?

SPECIFICATIONS OF YOUR CURRENT CLUBS	SPECIFICATIONS	COACH'S COMMENTS	DATE 27/10/04
IRONS			
Length – i.e. STD +1" etc.	+3/4"	Perfect	
Lie angle of head	1° Up	A little too flat	
Shaft flex	Stiff	Too stiff	
Shaft deflection point	High	Too high	
Shaft type – i.e. graphite – steel	Steel	OK	
Grip thickness	Standard	Too thin	
Set configuration i.e. 2 – Lob wedge	3–Lob wedge	OK	
WOODS			
Length of driver	45"	OK	
Length of fairway woods	+1/2"	OK	
Driver loft	9°	Too little loft	
Shaft flex	Stiff	Too stiff	
Shaft deflection point	High	Too high	
Shaft type – i.e. graphite – steel	Graphite	OK	
Grip thickness	Standard	Too thin	
Wood configuration i.e. 1–3–5	1–3	Required 5 wood	

Statistics don't lie

Do you actually know how well you drive the ball, hit your irons, pitch, chip, hit bunker shots or putt? Do you know how good you are in these areas or do you just think you know? In reality, very few people have an accurate idea of where they actually stand in relation to each facet of their game.

The only way that you can accurately assess your current level of ability is to keep some statistics and assess them over a period of ten rounds or more.

Statistics don't lie. While they may not be accurate if assessed over only one or two rounds, looking at statistics over a longer period will most certainly give you an accurate idea of the state of your golf game. Only after having established your current level of ability can you practise the aspects of your game most in need of work.

Keeping statistical information can give you a guide as to where your strengths and weaknesses actually lie. Although it only takes a few minutes to fill in your statistical records after a round of golf, you may struggle at first to remember each shot. After a while, remembering will become easier. You may even find it easier to keep your statistics while you play.

The round summary provided is quite a basic one, but we believe it to be adequate for the majority of golfers. You can make your own statistics chart to suit your needs if required. As with all information you are gathering, present the results to your coach for further discussion.

An example of how you should fill out your round summary sheet can be seen on the opposite page. Your complete set of ten round summary sheets is on pages 180–189 of Chapter 7. You can then summarise those ten rounds on page 190 and calculate your averages.

Sample – Round summary Golf course: *Royal Melb – W*   Date: *10/8/04*

	PAR	FAIRWAYS	GREENS	PITCHING	CHIPPING	BUNKERS	PUTTS	SCORE
1	4	Y (N)	Y (N)		1 ✗		2	5
2	5	(Y) N	(Y) N				2	5
3	4	(Y) N	Y (N)		1		1	4
4	5	Y (N)	Y (N)		1		1	5
5	3	Y N	(Y) N				2	3
6	4	Y (N)	Y (N)			1 ✔	1	4
7		(Y) N					1	3
8		(Y) N					2	4
9		(Y) N					2	4
10	4	(Y) N	(Y) N				2	4
11	4	(Y) N	Y (N)			1 ✗	2	5
12	5	(Y) N	(Y) N				2	5
13	3	Y N	Y (N)				2	4
14	4						2	6
15	5						2	5
16	3	Y N	Y (N)				2	4
17	4	Y (N)	Y (N)	1 ✔			1	4
18	4	(Y) N	Y (N)			1 ✗	2	5
Total	72	8	8	1 1	3 1	3 1	31	79

Callout notes:
- A chip is from the fringe of the green.
- Fairway in regulation is when your tee shot finishes on the mown fairway. This does not include par 3 holes.
- Green in regulation is when you are putting for a birdie or better.
- This statistic refers to greenside bunkers only.
- A pitch shot is anything less than a full swing but longer than a fringe chip.
- Your ball must be on the putting green to count as a putt.

Comment: *Hit it left all day*

4

Making your golf plan

Having completed a full analysis of your game, your coach can now determine where your strengths and weaknesses lie and start to put your golf plan together.

There are three elements to the plan:

• setting your goals

• creating your player's calendar

• making your golf time wheel

Goal setting

Your goals need to be specific and realistic, and you also need to set a date by which you want to achieve them. For example, you may have a current handicap of 21. One of your goals may be to get your handicap to 15 by a certain date. We recommend you give yourself a twelve-month period in which to achieve the target. If you don't have an official handicap, and your average score is say between 95 and 100, your goal may be to average between 90 and 95 or 85 to 90. Remember that your goals should be specific and realistic. You should keep your expectations in line with your efforts. If you plan to practise five times and play twice every week, your expectations should be understandably higher than if you plan to practise once a week and play once a fortnight.

Your coach should help you to set your goals. Remember your coach has done a thorough analysis of your golf game and will know what is realistic once you have determined how much time and effort you can afford to spend on your improvement.

At this point, the goals we are referring to are what we like to call **outcome goals**. These are goals that are outcome driven, such as lowering your handicap to a certain number by a certain date. These goals are essential to set if you wish to significantly improve your game. Your coach should then help you set what we call **process goals**. These goals detail the process required to achieve your outcome goals. They are the roadmap to your outcome goals. If you are travelling by car to a certain destination, your outcome goal would be to establish your destination before you take off in your vehicle. Your process goal would be reading the map to determine the best way to reach your destination.

An example of your goals chart can be seen on the opposite page. With your coach, you should write down your goals on pages 152–154 of Chapter 7.

Sample – Goal setting

DATE: 1/1/05

OUTCOME GOALS:

Lower handicap from 19 to 14 by 1/1/06.

Regularly break 90.

PROCESS GOALS:

Have a lesson with my coach every 3 weeks.

Set my time wheel and stick to it.

Change my grip from strong to neutral.

Practise swing plane to stop over the top movement.

Practise my chipping to get better feel.

Creating a player's calendar

Your player's calendar should be specifically designed around your personal needs. The red zone portion of the year is your rebuilding time, when only a small amount of time is spent playing golf on the course. We recommend that this period coincide with the winter months when the weather is poor. It's a time for working on your technique and getting your body in shape for golf. The green zone is a period of the year when less time is spent working on your technique and more time is spent actually playing golf. Remember, your player's calendar is designed around **your** desires and goals. The red zone, or off-season, is important if you genuinely wish to make changes to your technique. The player's calendar for you to fill out can be found on page 155.

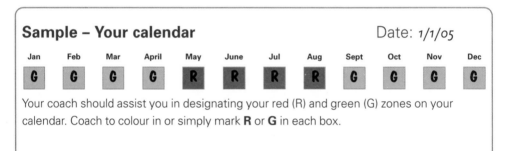

Sample – Your calendar   Date: *1/1/05*

Jan	Feb	Mar	April	May	June	Jul	Aug	Sept	Oct	Nov	Dec
G	G	G	G	R	R	R	R	G	G	G	G

Your coach should assist you in designating your red (R) and green (G) zones on your calendar. Coach to colour in or simply mark **R** or **G** in each box.

The red zone, or off-season, is important if you genuinely wish to make changes to your technique.

Sample – Player's calendar

The calendars below are examples only. Both you and your coach need to design a calendar specific to your requirements.

Beginner's calendar

The beginner may spend the first ten months of their golfing life in the red zone, focusing on technical practice and physical conditioning, with little on-course play.

Handicap golfer's calendar

Six months of the year may be devoted to game improvement (red zone), while the other six months could be heavily weighted towards playing golf in both social and competition play.

Elite golfer's calendar

The elite player may be engaged in competition and tournament play for eight months of the year (green zone) and have four months of game rebuilding time (red zone).

A question of balance – Golf time wheel

The game of golf can be broken down into five key areas:

TECHNICAL
Swing technique for all shots, including driver, fairway woods; long, mid and short irons; pitching; chipping; bunkers; and putting. Comprised of fundamentals such as grip, set-up, posture, alignment, pivot, swing plane, impact, balance and release.

MENTAL
Visualisation, concentration, determination, keeping the mind focused on the present and course management, as well as non-technical practice on the range.

PHYSICAL
Strength, balance, flexibility, endurance, co-ordination and speed.

GOLF PLAN
Your improvement framework illustrated in goals, playing calendar and golf time wheel.

PLAYING
Social play, competition play and tournament play.

To improve as a golfer you must take a balanced and holistic approach to the game by addressing all five areas. The time and effort you need to devote to each area will depend upon your competence in each of them. This decision is best made, not by you, but by your coach. The beginner golfer may spend the majority of his or her time on the technical aspects, with possibly some physical work, depending on his or her physical state, whereas the more advanced player may need to work more on the mental area.

We recommend that, with your coach, you devise a mid- to long-term development plan (say, one year), which can be modified accordingly as you make progress.

Taking this approach will help you avoid the very common trap of striving for technical perfection instead of becoming proficient in all areas, as are the world's best golf players. Equally, your technical expectations need to be in line with what your body is capable of doing.

The five key areas shown on the time wheel are divided for illustration purposes only. The configuration of the golf time wheel is proportional to the amount of time that should be devoted to each area. You and your coach should design a golf time wheel specific to your personal needs. Initial and re-evaluation wheels have been provided in Chapter 7 on pages 156–159.

Sample – Golf time wheel

It is very important to note that your golf time wheel may be as simple or as detailed in design as you and your coach wish to make it. You may want to divide up each of the five areas with intricate precision or, alternatively, use the golf time wheel as a more overall general guide to dividing up your golfing time.

Sample – Golf time wheels

RED ZONE

GOLF PLAN
PHYSICAL
PLAYING
TECHNICAL

GREEN ZONE

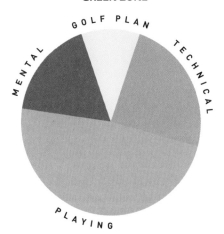

GOLF PLAN
TECHNICAL
MENTAL
PLAYING

Technical versus non-technical practice

While this explanation strictly belongs in Chapter 6 it has been brought forward for you to fully understand how the time wheel works.

The term non-technical practice refers to time you spend practising hitting any shot – from driving to putting – where you attempt to eliminate all conscious technical thought. It's a time to practise golf in a manner identical to the way you will play on the golf course when you incorporate your pre-shot routine.

Technical practice, on the other hand, is when you focus purely on the technical change you are working on, and disregard the flight of the ball. Most people make the mistake of returning to the course after a golf lesson from their coach thinking only about the technical changes. This is usually disastrous. Technical and non-technical practice should not be worked on together. Technical practice should only be carried out on the golf range, not on the course.

Motor learning experts claim that it takes a minimum of three weeks of daily practice for the subconscious mind to begin to accept a change. There is also evidence that it could

take between seven and fourteen months of regular practice for the re-patterning to become automatic.

We firmly believe that on a golf course swing-thoughts should be kept to a minimum or even completely non-existent during the execution of each shot. Most golfers will play their best when they clearly visualise the shot before executing it, and trust that their golf swing will produce the outcome they have imagined in their pre-shot routine.

This is one of the most important messages in this book. Understand the difference between technical practice and non-technical practice and forever practise them completely separately!

5

Let's get technical

Most people consider the technical side of golf to be of the greatest interest, importance and fun. What sheer joy it is to be confident with your grip, set-up and swing. That technical confidence provides the basis for consistent ball striking.

This part of the book will look the most similar to other instructional golf books, minus a lot of technical detail which your coach can provide if and when required. Areas covered include:

- grip
- set-up
- pivot
- plane
- release
- timing
- tempo
- pitching
- fringe chipping
- bunker shots
- putting

Set for success

GRIP

Grip pressure is a vital aspect of holding a golf club. Most people tend to strangle the handle of the golf club, creating tension in the wrist tendons and forearm muscles. This is the single biggest mistake anyone can make when swinging a golf club.

It's important to hold the club lightly, while keeping your upper body relaxed and athletically balanced.

The club should be held with a combination of palms and fingers running on a slight diagonal angle across both the palms and fingers of both hands. The Vs, formed between the index fingers and the thumb of each hand, should point towards your trailing shoulder or collar bone.

The illustrations, opposite, demonstrate what a right-handed golfer should see when looking down at his or her own grip, and when observing another golfer's grip.

The grip is important because it controls the club face. You should be able to lift your arms and club straight up and out in front of you, with no manipulation of the arms and wrists, to see that the leading edge of the club is vertical. This will influence the set-up as well as the plane of your swing. **An unorthodox grip will more than likely produce an unorthodox swing.**

We recommend that you make sure your grip is reasonably correct before you proceed to the next section of this book. Check that your coach is happy with your grip. You may need to spend a bit of time working on it to get it right.

You may have noticed that, at this point, there has been no mention of overlap, interlock or ten-finger grip styles. This is because these different ways of holding the club tend to have little influence over the things that are important, such as club face, set-up, swing plane, and so on. Experiment with your coach to work out which grip suits you best.

GRIP CHANGES

It's amazing how the slightest grip change can feel extremely strange. Making permanent changes can take some time and you will need to be diligent if you are to avoid reverting to your old habits, especially when you are under pressure.

Grip

Observing your own grip   **Observing another golfer's grip**

LESSON NOTES

The sample below highlights how pages 160–179 should be used during your lessons.

Sample – Lesson note

DATE: 1/11/04   (Circle area you are working on)

~~GRIP~~   SET-UP   ALIGNMENT   PIVOT   PLANE   RELEASE   PITCHING
CHIPPING   BUNKER   PUTTING   NON–TECH PRACTICE   COURSE MGT   MENTAL MGT

COACH CONCERNS
Left hand is far too weak.

SUGGESTED CHANGES
Move it across so that you can see two to three knuckles of the left hand.

DRILLS TO PRACTISE
Check it in a mirror regularly.

PLAYER'S REACTION
I am now drawing the ball.

SET-UP

A great golf swing is built around a great set-up. If your grip and set-up are sound, your chances of swinging the golf club effectively are substantially enhanced.

In a correct set-up position you should be perfectly balanced, with your weight evenly distributed on the balls of your feet. Watch a tennis player waiting to receive a serve, a guard on a basketball court or a soccer goal–

keeper. All these activities are best performed while the athlete is equally balanced on the balls of his or her feet.

You need to bend forwards from the hips and slightly flex your knees to create a minimal curve in the spine. Make sure not to tuck your chin in, and be sure to let your arms hang freely. The correct distance from the ball should be determined by correct posture and the length of the club.

Because the trailing hand sits below the leading hand on the grip, the trailing shoulder should naturally be lower than the leading shoulder. In turn, this allows the base of the spine to slide slightly towards the target while the top of the spine moves equally in the opposite direction.

The ball position should be slightly forward of centre when using short irons, a little forward of that when using mid and long irons, just inside the leading heel when using fairway woods, and opposite the leading heel when using the driver.

Correct ball position may vary depending on your golf swing. Our suggested ball positions are recommendations only. Your coach will determine the correct ball position for your swing.

ALIGNMENT

It's important to align the face of the golf club directly with the intended target. To do this, align the leading edge of the club face at 90 degrees to the target line. You should then place your feet into position so that if you ran a line along the toes they would be parallel to the target line. It's similar to standing on a train track with your ball and club face on one track and your feet on the other.

By far the majority of weekend golfers misalign themselves in the set-up. To avoid this problem lie a club on the ground when you are practising to assist with correct alignment. This can be seen in the illustrations on the next page. By placing a club on the ground in practice your eyes will adjust to accept what correct alignment really looks like. Doing this regularly will ensure it will become automatic on the golf course.

If your alignment is correct your golf swing won't require any manipulations or compensations to propel the ball towards the target. Conversely, if you misaim you will subconsciously make compensations within your golf swing as you attempt to hit the ball to the intended target. In short, correct alignment will encourage a balanced and compensation-free golf swing.

Distance from the ball – Alignment

Pitching wedge

Driver

250

Placing a club on the ground parallel to your target line
will help you develop good alignment habits.

Ball position

When using a wedge, the best position for the ball is centre or just forward of centre. When using a driver, the ball is often played inside the leading heel. These are recommendations only.

Pitching wedge   **Driver**

The mysterious Ps

We like to call pivot and plane 'the mysterious Ps' because so few people seem to understand these two areas. We will outline the very basics, but your coach should be the judge as to whether you require more knowledge in these areas.

PIVOT

Pivot is the term used to describe the movement of the body during the golf swing. Pivot refers to everything except the arms and golf club. Correct pivot is essential to creating a sound and repetitive arm plane, shoulder plane, and club shaft plane.

Essentially, a correct pivot relies upon a sound set-up. It would be unwise to work on your pivot from a poor set-up position. Don't proceed until your coach has signed off on your grip and set-up, as mentioned in the previous section of this chapter.

As you can see in the illustrations on pages 56 and 60, the spine is tilted in two directions in the correct set-up position – forwards toward the ball and slightly sideways to allow the trailing hand to sit below the leading hand in the grip. The objective is to retain these angles until the

top of the backswing, with little, if any, shift in angles. The illustrations on pages 56–63 highlight the positions of the body during the pivot. The left-hand image on each page illustrates what is commonly known as the pivot drill. This pivot drill can be performed as an exercise to develop and learn the skills of the correct pivot action. It has been placed alongside corresponding positions in the swing to highlight the relevance of this drill to the golf swing. The dotted line highlights the angle of the upper body. Looking at the first set of these illustrations on pages 56–59, you will notice that the angle of the upper body has been maintained until the top of the backswing. The upper body tilt, or angle, then increases in the downswing by virtue of the lower body shifting laterally in the downswing.

When viewing illustrations on pages 60–63, you can see that the forward tilt of the spine is maintained from the set-up position through to impact and then almost to the finish of the swing.

It's important to note that for consistent ball contact you need to maintain these angles, at least until impact. If, after impact, you have a tendency to stand more upright, the effect will be minimal provided you maintain balance.

During the pivot your shoulders turn approximately at a right angle or 90 degrees to the spine. The importance of correct shoulder movement will become increasingly obvious when we discuss the planes of the swing.

In the illustrations on page 57 you can see the weight shift onto the trailing foot during the backswing. It's important to note that there should be no deliberate lateral hip movement to shift the weight. It's purely a function of the body turning. There's a common misconception that to shift your weight onto the trailing foot during the backswing you need to slide your hips away from the target. This type of movement creates what is commonly known as a reverse pivot. It is, in fact, unnecessary.

Think of it this way. At address, the upper body sits predominantly over the lower body, therefore resulting in a balanced set-up. With a correct backswing, the shoulders and – to a lesser degree – the hips, should rotate, allowing the upper body to be stacked over the trailing leg. The result of this is that roughly three-quarters of your body mass is situated behind the ball, resulting in the perfect weight shift. Again it's important to stress that correct weight shift occurs without any lateral movement of the hips.

The less you turn your hips, and the more you turn your shoulders, the greater the coil. It should be difficult to hold this top backswing position for any length of time, causing the downswing to commence instinctively. Your hips should move slightly towards the target during the downswing, causing you to slightly increase the angle of your spine and transfer your body weight forward to your leading leg. People with a lack of flexibility will require more hip turn in the backswing than those who are more flexible.

To allow the pivot action to occur naturally and correctly, you should rotate your head slightly. By allowing your head to swivel naturally during the backswing your body will rotate correctly.

Comparing the pivot to the swing

The spine is tilted slightly due to the trailing hand being positioned below the leading hand as you grip the club.

**In the backswing, weight shift is purely a function
of the body turning.**

Comparing the pivot to the swing (cont'd)

The downswing consists of a lateral
hip shift, allowing weight to shift to
the leading leg.

The angle of the spine is slightly
increased due to the lateral
hip movement.

A balanced and fully rotated finishing position shows only the point of the trailing shoe on the ground.

Comparing the pivot to the swing (cont'd)

**Two bends – one from the knees and one from the hips.
The weight should be balanced on the balls of the feet.**

The shoulders essentially turn around the spine.

Comparing the pivot to the swing (cont'd)

At impact the trailing heel is slightly off the ground and the hips are partially rotated, showing how dynamic a good golf swing should be.

**The body is in a slightly more vertical position at the finish of the swing.
Good balance in the finishing position is very important.**

PLANE

The swing plane can be easily misunderstood as it is quite a complex subject. It's not essential for most golfers to fully understand the intricacies of the swing plane. Many elite sports people don't fully understand the physics and biomechanics of their particular skills. They tend to have a sound general knowledge of the movements required in their chosen sport, and have an ability to perform these actions correctly, smoothly, gracefully and almost instinctively.

The plane of the swing is a reasonably complicated aspect of the golf swing, largely because it is three-dimensional. **Simply put, swing plane refers to the direction in which the arms and hands swing, as well as the orbit of the club head during the golf swing.**

This is where your coach is essential. If your coach considers your swing plane to be of concern, then learning more about it will enhance your chances of improvement. On the other hand, if your coach is happy with your plane, leave it alone. As they say, 'if it ain't broke, don't fix it'.

There is an old saying, 'plane is king', meaning plane is important. It's important because it will determine the direction from which the club head will attack the ball. Plane will have an enormous bearing on the flight of the golf ball. Remember, correct swing plane should be a reasonably natural occurrence.

Looking at the series of illustrations showing the swing sequence on pages 70–73, you can see that the head of the club is swung upon an incline or angular plane. It's clear that the club head is not swinging along the target line and the face of the club does not always point at the target.

Many golfers incorrectly think that the club head should be swung in a straight line directly away from the target in the backswing, and then down and straight through to the target in the through swing. They may also think that the face of the club should stay facing the target during the swing, the same way it does in the set-up position. This way of thinking will almost certainly result in a poor swing plane.

The illustrations on pages 66–67 show a golfer hitting a golf ball off an imaginary high tee located at around chest height. This is essentially a golf swing on a horizontal plane. It is obviously a similar movement to that of a baseballer. In the illustrations it's clear that the face of the club does not stay pointing towards the target during the swing. It appears to open in the backswing and close during the through swing.

Try some swings for yourself, imagining that the ball is out in front of you at around chest height. Observe how the club face naturally wants to rotate both in the backswing and the through swing. The only time the face of the club

should be pointing at the target is at address and impact. It's important not to think you should deliberately rotate the club back and through. It will do this automatically, by virtue of the trailing arm folding and the wrists hinging in the backswing, and the leading arm folding and the wrists hinging again in the through swing.

In a golf swing, the club head is swung in a circular pattern on an incline plane with the face of the club continually rotating. Remember, your coach is the best judge of how much knowledge and understanding you need to have on the subject of the swing plane.

Simply put, swing plane refers to the direction in which the arms and hands swing, as well as the orbit of the club head during the golf swing.

The baseball drill

Notice that the shaft of the golf club stays within the shaded area. Like a golf swing, the plane is not singular. There is a band of tolerance to move within.

Performing this baseball drill will assist you in understanding the basic mechanics of the swing plane.

SWING PLANE'S CONE OF CONFIDENCE

The swing plane has suggested parameters which are clearly shown by the cone of confidence in this illustration.

Because swing plane is a complicated science, these boundaries are suggested guidelines only. Opinions vary when it comes to this subject, so your coach is an extremely important person to refer to when working on your plane.

Looking at the illustrations on the following pages, note the bottom edge of the cone that runs directly up the club shaft. This is referred to as shaft plane. The upper edge, that runs from the bottom of the shaft up through the trailing shoulder, is referred to as the shoulder plane.

In an ideal world, the club shaft would remain on or within the boundaries of the cone throughout the entire golf swing. **Most of history's great golfers have had their hands in line with the shoulder plane when the club is at the top of the backswing.** For many of them, the entire club shaft also sits on this plane.

Like all fundamentals relating to the golf swing, these are just parameters to work within and there is no one absolutely perfect series of positions. Your coach will assist you in fine-tuning your swing positions to suit your tendencies.

The slightly complicated issue is that even when the shaft of the club stays on or within the cone of confidence during the entire swing, it doesn't mean you have it all working correctly. There are preferred positions to achieve within the cone during the course of the golf swing. Again, your coach is your best form of reference.

Unlike most other instructional books, we have not attempted to detail the many intricacies of the swing plane. We have chosen to do this for two reasons:

- There is no absolutey correct or ideal swing plane.
- Your coach will determine where your swing plane should be due to your particular circumstances.

CORRECT PLANE IS A NATURAL OCCURRENCE

As mentioned, the edge of the cone running through the shoulders at set-up (shoulder plane) is the ideal position to be in when the club is at the top of the backswing. Try the throwing drill demonstrated in the illustrations on pages 74–75.

These illustrations show the natural role of the trailing arm in the golf swing, demonstrated by a throwing action. Ideally, the trailing arm should control the swing. It's very important to note the relationship between the trailing hand, trailing shoulder and the ball located on the ground in the throwing illustration 3 on page 75. The positioning of the body and the trailing arm are identical to the correct top of the backswing position. The point to note is how natural and easy this position is to find when throwing a ball.

As previously mentioned, swing plane is a complicated subject and your coach is the best person to explain this to you in greater detail.

Most of history's golfers have had their hands in line with the shoulder plane when the club is at the top of the backswing.

Cone of confidence

**The shaded area defined by the shaft and shoulder planes
is what we call the cone of confidence.**

Shaft

Shoulder

Plane

Plane

③ ④

**At the top of the swing it is ideal to have the hands
and the club shaft sitting on the shoulder plane.**

Cone of confidence (cont'd)

⑤ To hit the golf ball straight, the shaft of the club should be within and parallel to the band of tolerance at all times.

⑥ The shaft of the club does not necessarily need to return to its address position at impact.

⑦   ⑧

The only time the shaft of the club should be outside the cone is during the finish with the hands approximately on the shoulder plane.

Throwing drill

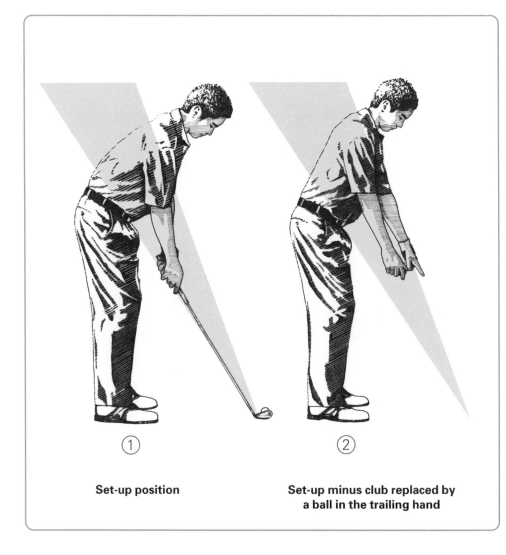

①

Set-up position

②

Set-up minus club replaced by a ball in the trailing hand

③
Top of throwing position

④
Throwing release

Let it go

The term 'release' is used to describe the correct use of the forearms, wrists and golf club, throughout the golf swing. In particular, it refers to positions shortly before, during and after impact with the ball. It's about using the wrists and the forearms in a way that accelerates the club head so that it reaches its fastest point at impact. To do this, you use the continuous rotational movement of the body in synchronisation with the arms, wrists and club. It's not about manipulating the club head. It's about letting it go.

Correct release of the club contributes to much of the club head speed required to hit the golf ball great distances. **Correct release of the club explains how seemingly small, weak-looking people can hit the golf ball a long way, while some musclemen struggle to hit it out of their shadow**.

Correct release begins in the backswing, where the trailing arm should fold to allow the trailing wrist to bend. This creates an angle between the leading arm and shaft of around 90 degrees. As the body and arms begin to swing down towards the ball, the angle between the leading arm and the club shaft should remain about the same or become slightly more acute before gradually opening up, so that at impact with the ball only a small angle remains.

This movement is heavily controlled by the trailing arm straightening at the correct time in the downswing. This causes the club head to accelerate as it approaches impact and creates a slight downward blow to the ball, particularly with the irons. With mid and shorter irons, a divot should appear under the ball or even slightly forward of the ball, depending on how the ball lies on the ground.

The illustrations on pages 78–79 show an ideal release of the golf club. This is effortless power. **It's important to understand that this is not a manufactured motion. If a minimum of grip pressure is applied to the club during the swing, the club head should lag behind the hands in the downswing, allowing a 'cracking of a whip' type effect at impact, delivering the club head into the impact with immense power.** It's so easy to get caught up in trying to control the club head.

Releasing the club correctly is a facet of the golf swing that very few golfers do well. Master this and you will find that golf is a far easier game to play.

The intangible Ts

We like to call timing and tempo 'the intangible Ts' because they are elements of the swing which are purely derived from feel.

Timing is the term used to describe the co-ordination or sequencing of the body, arms, wrists and club. Tempo is the speed at which all this occurs.

TIMING

Timing will vary from one golfer to another, due to differences in swing mechanics, ball position, strength and flexibility, as well as golf club specifications. As a result, timing is a subject best discussed with your coach. In general, the better your golf swing, the less it will rely upon timing for consistency.

For deficient golf swings, the timing or sequencing of the body, arms, wrists and club is vital. These manipulations and compensations occur at a subconscious level to create an impact condition with the ball reasonable enough to send the ball roughly in the right direction.

The problem with playing golf this way is that the timing you rely upon so heavily tends to desert you in important pressure situations. This explains why many weekend golfers often play practice rounds quite well by their standards and then play quite poorly in important competitions, such as club championships and trophy events. Their central nervous system just can't cope with the added pressure, so they are unable to reproduce their complicated and intricate timing. If your swing mechanics are sound, your golf swing will stand up more readily under the pressure of competition golf.

TEMPO

Tempo is the speed at which the golf swing is performed. **History shows us that there have been great golfers with fast swings and great golfers with slow swings. Tempo can be effective when it is quick or slow.**

Generally speaking, a person who talks and eats quickly will swing the golf club with a more upbeat tempo than someone who does those activities slowly. In short, your tempo should match your personality and feel comfortable for you.

History shows us that there have been great golfers with fast swings and great golfers with slow swings. Tempo can be effective when it is quick or slow.

Full swing release

The angle between the leading arm and club gradually opens approaching impact.

The hands are slightly ahead of the club head at impact, facilitating maximum power.

Approach shots

Approach shots, commonly known as pitching, refer to shots that are further out from the hole than a chip shot around the green, but are less than a full shot. In order to become proficient at this shot, a sound technique and a lot of practice are required. **It's a similar action to a full swing, however, the swing must be abbreviated to suit the length of the shot at hand.** Like chipping, it's possible to pitch with a variety of clubs, depending on the lie; conditions such as wind; and the pin placement upon the green. Generally, the wedges are used for best results.

Some things to note:

- The shorter the pitch, the narrower the stance, with the opposite being true for long pitch shots.
- For a standard pitch shot the ball position should be central.
- Grip slightly down the handle of the club for added control.
- Like chipping and putting, the length of swing, and therefore the club head speed, will regulate the distance the ball travels through the air.
- The plane of the pitching swing is the same as explained for the full swing. There is a point at which a chip shot

becomes a pitch shot. In essence, a chip is predominantly a one-lever motion whereas a pitch is a two-lever motion. **In layman's terms, this means that a chip shot should be played predominantly without the use of the wrists, while a pitching motion requires a definite contribution from the wrists.**

To understand the basics of levers, it could be said that the primary lever in the golf swing is the leading arm, whether you are putting, chipping, pitching, playing from a bunker or taking a full swing. The secondary lever is the movement of the leading wrist, which can act as a gear and multiply the speed of the club head.

Because a chip shot is played from close to the green edge, and the objective of the shot is to land the ball onto the edge of the green and allow it to release up to the hole, the distance you need to carry the ball through the air is minimal. As a result, a reasonably small swing is required that demands little or no wrist activity. Conversely, when a slightly longer carry is required, a naturally longer swing is needed, which will encourage some wrist movement.

For short pitch shots, the body weight should be predominantly on the leading leg, progressively becoming more centred as the pitch shot becomes longer. This is because at impact the best position for your weight and hands is slightly forward. For chipping and short pitches, the swing is too small to allow

time for the weight to move onto the trailing foot in the backswing and back to the correct position at impact. On longer pitch shots, however, like a full swing, the golf swing is long enough to allow time for the weight to shift back to the trailing foot during the backswing and then to the leading foot by the time the golf ball is struck.

Controlling the distance of your pitch shots is what good pitching is all about. A simple way to improve this aspect of your game is to purchase three or four plastic cones or witches' hats, find an area on the practice range or in a park where you can place the hats at various distances and pitch to them. For example, you could place the hats at 30, 40, 50 and 60 metres away from you and practise hitting shots to each of those targets. At your next practice session you could place the hats at 35, 45, 55 and 65 metres away. This type of practice is extremely beneficial for lowering your scores on the course as it encourages you to develop an instinctive feel for shots of various distances.

Pitching

Ball position should be around the centre of the stance.

Like the full swing, the hands should slightly lead the club head at impact.

Pitching (cont'd)

Grip down the handle of the club for added control.

Impact looks similar to address.

Off the edge

The term 'off the edge' refers to what is commonly known as a fringe chip. This is a shot played usually within about 10 metres of the edge of the putting green. Regardless of ability, we all miss some greens in regulation. In fact, it's crucial for most golfers to be proficient at this part of the game, as you'll need to chip on several holes during a round of golf. A well-executed chip can result in a putt from short range. This can make up for a poor drive or approach shot to the green. **How wonderful it is to receive the praise from a playing partner, 'Great up and down'. The soul mate of chipping is putting. These are two combined shots based on skill and imagination, where age and strength matter little.** Both require as much, if not more practice than the full swing. The reasons are simple.

Short game improvement will improve your score far more quickly than long game improvement. They are the shots that really help or hurt your score.

When changing the distance you wish to hit the golf ball with the full swing, you simply change clubs. For example, if tour players want to hit the ball 150 metres they may use a 7 iron. If instead they wish to hit the ball 160 metres, rather than changing the swing, they will choose a 6 iron. The length, speed and style of the swing remains constant. However, this is not the case with the short game. Using a variety of clubs with different swing lengths allows you to control both the carry and the distance the ball will roll when it hits the green. The imagination required to 'see' the vast array of shots can only be built up over time as you hone your skills for each type of shot.

It's important to note that as a backswing becomes longer, the club head speed naturally increases during the downswing, so a longer chipping swing will naturally produce a faster head speed at impact than a shorter one.

CLUB SELECTION

For fringe chipping, club selection is an inexact science. Some good players favour chipping with a favourite club and many chip with a variety of different clubs. There is no definitive answer, except to say that beginners should always look to play the 'low–risk' percentage style of shot until their skill level allows them to hit 'higher–risk' shots with confidence.

The safest approach is to land the ball onto the putting surface and get the ball running as soon as possible. By way of example, a high–risk shot would involve using a lofted club and carrying the ball all the way to the flag in an endeavour to make the ball stop quickly. In contrast, the less advanced golfer should land the ball not far onto the putting surface with a less lofted club, so that the ball can run up towards the hole. This low–risk shot has a greater chance of repeated success, especially when you are under pressure. Equally, a slight miss-hit with a less lofted club will usually still produce a reasonable result, while the opposite is true for the more lofted high-risk shot.

Sometimes you may have no choice but to use a lofted club because of the lack of green to roll the ball on between you and the hole.

CHIPPING TECHNIQUE

The following fundamentals are recommended when chipping:

- Grip the golf club slightly down the handle for added control.
- Stand with your feet close together.
- Bend forward from the tops of the legs, unlocking the knees.
- Place the ball in the centre of your stance, or slightly behind the centre.
- Placing the ball off-centre in your stance has the effect of opening the club face. To combat this, simply open the stance enough to re-square the club face.
- Angle the knees, body weight and hands slightly forward. This should result in most of your body weight being on your leading leg.
- Keep your body weight predominantly on the leading side during the swing. Swing the arms, club and shoulders back and through as a unit. A minimum of wrist action is required for this shot. In some ways, the action is similar to a putt. In general, the longer the chip shot, the more wrist action, while for a shorter chip shot, less wrist action is required.

A lofted chip with a lofted club, such as a sand wedge

A running chip with a less lofted club, such as a 7 iron

Chipping

Hands and weight slightly forward at address.

A small chip requires little, if any, wrist action.

Impact is similar to address.

The finish consists of little, if any, wrist action.

Chipping (cont'd)

Stance slightly open in the set-up position.

Impact is similar to address.

The length of the follow-through is similar to the length of the backswing.

Bunkered

Playing a shot from a greenside bunker is different to playing any other shot in golf because the objective is to strike the ground behind the ball rather than hitting the ball first. In other words, you are intentionally trying to duff the shot. It is for this very reason that shots from greenside sand often make the weekend golfer feel 'bunkered' and nervous. To hit a bunker shot a distance of 10 metres, you need to make a swing that would send a ball about four times that distance if it was being hit from the fairway. Because the club should hit the sand 5 to 8 cm behind the ball, the sand restricts the speed of the club. The face of the club should never actually make contact with the ball. The golf ball will come out of the bunker on top of a slice of sand, landing safely upon the green.

The difficulty with this shot is that the subconscious mind knows that to make the golf ball travel a long way, a long, powerful swing is required. Conversely, it thinks that to hit the ball a short distance, a shorter, softer swing at the ball is required. Because of this, it's very important to practise your swing outside the bunker before you enter it to make sure you commit to exactly the length and speed of the swing required.

Although techniques for bunker shots vary a little from one great player to the next, some recommended suggestions are listed below for a standard shot from a good lie. They are portrayed in the illustrations on pages 96–101.

- Always first assess the way the ball lies in the bunker. This will primarily determine how the shot needs to be played.
- Shuffle your feet into the sand a little at address. This will give you a solid footing, as well as an idea of what the sand is like under the surface. It's important to know whether the sand is hard or soft, wet or dry, shallow or deep, and so on.
- Take a reasonably wide stance, at least as wide as you would with your driver.
- Flex the knees a little more than with other shots, to help you stabilise your lower body.
- Grip down the club a little.
- Beginners are advised to set up with the club face square. More advanced players should slightly open the face, in which case the stance should also be slightly open.

- The path of the club should swing in relation to the line of your feet. Often when an average player opens the face and stance, they make the mistake of swinging back and through towards the target, instead of committing to the line of the feet.

- The bunker shot swing technique is very similar to a high, soft landing lob shot, or pitch shot. There should be no excessive picking up of the club, nor should there be any more wrist cock than for a pitch shot.

- The length of the backswing should by and large mirror the length of the follow-through.

- The length of the swing should regulate the distance the ball travels, in a similar way to a pitch shot. A shorter shot requires a short swing, while the opposite is true for a slightly longer bunker shot.

- Aim to hit the sand somewhere between 5 to 8 cm behind the ball, taking a relatively shallow slice of sand out of the bunker.

GENERAL RULES OF THUMB FOR OTHER LIES

- Buried lies are a slightly more difficult shot to execute. Simply put, you must hit down into the sand, taking a deeper divot of sand out of the bunker. This will prevent the back edge or 'bounce' on the sole of the club from bouncing off the sand. **The more severely the ball is buried, the more severely the club head should descend into the sand.**

- In particularly soft sand, the club will be slowed down more by the sand, so more swing, and therefore more club head speed, is required.

- In hard or wet sand, the club will tend to bounce more and not dig in as much, so you need less swing, and therefore less club head speed.

- When the ball is sitting in a depression in the sand or it is just a poor lie in general, a slightly more descending blow is required than for a standard lie. The worse the lie, the more the shot should be played like a buried lie. Talk to your coach regarding these different types of lies.

Greenside bunker shot

A wide stance creates a stable base. An open club face is suitable for most bunker shots.

The lower body remains very stable.

Very similar to a pitch shot backswing.

The club head slides under the ball.

Greenside bunker shot (cont'd)

A quiet and stable lower body.

**The length of the follow-through is
similar to that of the length of the backswing.**

**Because of the open club face,
the stance is open to the target.**

**It is essential to swing the club outside
the plane with a bunker shot.**

Greenside bunker shot (cont'd)

The club is swung back and through in relation to the line of the feet, not the target line.

The club head should strike around 5–8 cm behind the ball.

**The club face remains
open after impact.**

Very little leg action is required.

Putt for dough

There's an old saying that goes 'drive for show and putt for dough', which gives you some idea of the importance of good putting. The putting stroke is the smallest of all golf swings, so it makes sense that it should be the simplest of actions.

Putting is comprised of three main principles:

- **reading the green**
- **direction**
- **distance control**

It really is that simple. **If you can read the green correctly, aim the putter face in the intended direction and send the ball on the desired line with the right speed, it will go into the hole.** Only such things as unexpected gusts of wind or imperfections in the green can cause the putt to miss.

READING THE GREEN

'Reading the green' is all about surveying the lie of the land. It's about deciding where the high and low points of the green are. Is your putt uphill, left to right, right to left, or a combination of all of the above? Is there grain in the green? This is when the grass grows on an angle,

influencing the ball's line and speed. Grain is usually most evident in humid climates.

One thing is for certain, just as you can't learn to ride a bicycle by reading a book, you can't learn to read a green in the same manner. Like riding a bike, it takes a few goes before you find that perfect balance. It's unlikely that anyone will ever perfect the art of reading the green; however, you'll find that the skill required to predict the line a ball must travel upon a putting green will improve dramatically with practice. Spending some time during your lessons with your coach on the golf course will enable you to ask questions about reading the greens.

A good image to conjure up in your head is one where you throw a bucket of water onto the green. Which way will the water trickle? Whatever you imagine the water doing is the same as the ball will do.

The majority of golfers under-read their putts. By this we mean that most golfers don't read enough break into the putt when assessing the lie of the land. By way of example, if a golfer needs to aim the ball to start 1 metre to the right of the hole, most players read the putt thinking that they need to aim half a metre to the right of the hole. This is known as having 'under-read the putt'. If you miss your putt on the low side by under-reading, it's commonly known as missing on the 'amateur side' of the hole. Putts missed on the high side are known as missing on the 'pro side'. This is because amateurs most often miss on the low side and pros are more prone to miss their putts on the 'high side'.

DIRECTION

Direction relies on correct green reading. Once this has been achieved, directional control is influenced by three things:

* **putter face alignment**
* **putting set-up**
* **the putting stroke**

Putter face alignment

It's crucial to develop good habits when it comes to putter face alignment, as poor alignment is a great hindrance to your putting stroke. **Although most golfers assume their putter face alignment is reasonably good, in general, this is not the case.** As the ability to aim the face of the putter on the intended line is an essential and quite difficult skill to develop, you need to check your putter face alignment regularly.

Your coach will want to check your putter face alignment. It can be done with a laser designed for this specific purpose or with a plastic triangle placed against the face of your putter at address. If neither of these devices is available to you, place a credit card from your wallet lengthways against the face of your putter after you have aligned a putt, and walk back a few paces to view the direction in which you've aimed. It's best to have a friend do this for you as it's difficult to bend over to place the credit card against the face of the putter without the putter head moving from its original position.

We recommend that you fill in the putter face alignment chart on page 136 of Chapter 7, to keep a check on your putter face alignment. You should regularly check to see how accurately you align the putter face. Using the chart over the page, align your putter face around 3 metres from the hole and have a friend or your coach place a triangle or credit card against the face of your putter. Do this five times each time you perform this test and place five ticks in the appropriate boxes. The data accumulated will assist you in understanding your tendencies when it comes to aligning your putter face. Your coach will give you drills to assist you in better aligning your putter face.

Sample – Putter face alignment chart

Test (✔) to be repeated five times on each date.

DATE	ALIGNMENT OUTSIDE LEFT EDGE	ALIGNMENT LEFT EDGE	ALIGNMENT STRAIGHT	ALIGNMENT RIGHT EDGE	ALIGNMENT OUTSIDE RIGHT EDGE
6/10/04	✔ ✔ ✔	✔ ✔			
7/11/04	✔ ✔	✔ ✔	✔		
5/12/04	✔	✔ ✔	✔ ✔		
8/1/05		✔	✔ ✔ ✔	✔	

Putting set-up – the grip

Unlike almost all other shots in golf, the putter should be held in the palms of the hands with the thumbs placed on the top of the grip. You will notice that the top of the putter grip is flat. It's been specifically designed for this purpose. As for almost all shots in golf, the putter should be held nice and lightly.

As a starting point, the back of the leading hand and the palm of the trailing hand should face the intended starting line of the golf ball, although in our opinion the way the putter is held is less important than any other club.

Observing the greatest putters in history highlights the many weird and wonderful ways that the putter can successfully be held. Some of the various ways in which you can hold the club include a conventional style grip – where the trailing hand sits below the leading hand on the grip of the putter – and a cross hand or reverse grip method – where the opposite occurs. There is no real right or wrong way to hold a putter or right or wrong type of putter to use – just whatever works best for you. This is where your coach has the experience and knowledge to steer you in the right direction.

The putting stroke

For any golf shot, think of your body as being a machine that swings a golf club. The machine must start in the correct position and, just as importantly, it must start in the same position each time for a consistent outcome.

The putting stroke should be similar to that of the pendulum motion of an antique clock. The shape formed between the two arms and the putter shaft should resemble the letter 'Y'. Swinging the Y shape without any use of the wrists helps create a pendulum-type motion. Excessive use of the wrists creates a distance control problem because like the full swing, wrist action creates club head speed. The correct set-up should consist of having your:

- feet approximately shoulder width apart for stability
- weight on the balls of your feet
- upper body bent forward from the hips so your eyes are over the ball
- arms hanging freely
- hands level with or slightly forward of the ball
- shoulder and forearm alignment parallel to the intended line upon which the golf ball will start

DISTANCE CONTROL

Controlling the distance that your golf ball travels on the putting green is crucial to great putting. Distance control is only possible on the putting green if you consistently hit the ball in the centre of the putter face. To achieve good distance control, you must have a sound putting technique.

Remember that the length of the back stroke should somewhat resemble the length of the through stroke. The longer the stroke, the more momentum, therefore the more club head speed. In general terms, this means a short putting stroke will create less club head speed than a longer one, producing a shorter roll of the golf ball. Your coach will give you distance control putting drills to help you become proficient in this area.

Putting

**The arms and shoulders moving together help the
wrists stay passive during the stroke.**

The length of the backswing resembles the length of the follow-through.

Putting (cont'd)

At set-up, the feet, knees, hips, shoulders and forearms should all be aligned parallel to each other.

The body remains steady during the stroke.

6

Managing your mind and emotions

Once a golfer has achieved a fundamentally sound technique in all areas of the game, managing the mind and emotions is the next critical step to continued game improvement. Golf is a game where technical excellence will guarantee success, only when it is accompanied by a cool and calculating mind.

Take control

The mental or psychological area of golf can be divided up into three parts:

- **non-technical practice**
- **course management**
- **mental focus**

All three parts have a major impact on your ability to play golf to a proficient level.

Non-technical practice is time spent practising without any conscious technical thought. It is critical not only to understand the distinction between technical and non-technical practice but to adhere to it at all times. Refer back to pages 44–45 for a detailed explanation.

Course management refers to how you plot yourself around the golf course. Good course management helps you to make rational, calculated decisions based upon knowing your strengths and weaknesses.

Mental focus refers to what is commonly known as 'being in the zone'. It means blocking out all distractions, to focus solely on things such as ball, target line and target. You need to think positively and stay in the present moment, with no thoughts of the past or future that might generate anxiety.

These three elements combined will have a serious effect on the scores you post and, ultimately, your handicap.

Course management

Being able to hit the golf ball solidly and consistently in play is obviously a major requisite for being an accomplished golfer. While there is no doubt that sound technique in all facets of the game is important, plotting your way around the golf course effectively is just as important. **Golf can be likened to a game of chess, as you strategically endeavour to plot your way around a myriad of trees, rough, bunkers, water hazards and out-of-bounds fences.**

As every golf course is different it's impossible to cover every possible situation that you may encounter when playing this great game. As a result, consult your coach with any questions you may have. Playing with your coach in a lesson environment is the best way to learn more about course management. It's an area of the game which is largely ignored by the average player. You can easily shave many strokes off the scorecard by making an effort to think your way around a golf course. Consider the following ideas to help you lower your score.

KNOW YOUR HOME COURSE

How well do you know your home course? Does it have 100, 150, 200 metre distance markers? If so, are these measurements to the front or centre of the greens? If not, have you measured any landmarks such as bunker edges, sprinkler heads or large trees to the front or centre of the greens? Do you know the carry-over of certain obstacles, such as bunkers, from the tee? How far is it through the fairway on dogleg holes? How far is it from the tee to where the fairway is widest or narrowest? These are examples of questions you should be asking yourself.

The following diagram shows how your own homemade yardage book should look. This is, of course, only one hole and you will need to chart all 18. Your book should be made small enough to fit into your back pocket along with your scorecard.

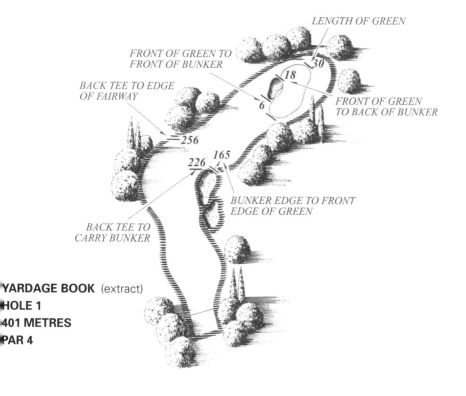

LENGTH OF GREEN

FRONT OF GREEN TO
FRONT OF BUNKER

BACK TEE TO EDGE
OF FAIRWAY

18

30

6

FRONT OF GREEN
TO BACK OF BUNKER

256

165

226

BUNKER EDGE TO FRONT
EDGE OF GREEN

BACK TEE TO
CARRY BUNKER

YARDAGE BOOK (extract)
HOLE 1
401 METRES
PAR 4

Having a golf course measured in this way gives you a distinct advantage, as it removes all the guesswork. It should only take a very short time to work out any distance and you will be rewarded by a great boost in your confidence over your club selection and where you choose to hit the ball.

Of course, having a golf course well mapped out is only an advantage if you know how far you hit each club under still, normal conditions. This is not learned at the driving range using range balls to poorly measured targets. It's best done out on the golf course, usually during practice rounds. Remember, par 3 holes are measured from the back tee to the centre of the green. Comparing how far you hit certain clubs against the length of the hole will assist you in learning how far you hit with each club.

Taking it one step further, learn to pace in metres. Again, this is best done on par 3 holes by walking from the back tee to the centre of the green and counting your steps. Compare the number of steps taken to the stated length of the golf hole. If you counted more steps than the length of the hole shows, you must lengthen your stride to pace in metres and, of course, vice versa if you count less steps. Learning to pace in metres makes it easier for you to accurately measure how far you hit each club on any hole – not just par 3s.

You should re-measure your distances periodically, as improvement to your golf swing will more than likely increase the distance you are capable of hitting with each club. This should also always be done after you purchase new equipment.

Now you have the golf course mapped out and you know how far you hit with each club, use this information to your advantage. Almost all golfers come up short when approaching the green with their iron shots, mostly because the majority of golfers make their club selection by eye and don't use measurements, let alone have an accurate idea of how far they can hit each club.

Remember, also, to take the following variables into account:

TEE MARKERS AND PIN PLACEMENTS

The positioning of the tee markers and pins influences the distance a golf hole will play. In other words, if both the tee markers and the pin positions are forward the hole will play shorter than the distance on the scorecard. Remember that golf holes are measured from the back tee to the centre of the green. The positioning of tee markers makes a big difference on par 3 holes in particular.

WIND

The wind can affect your golf ball quite considerably. When hitting into the wind the golf ball will fly a shorter distance. If you are a low ball hitter your ball will be less affected by a headwind than if you are a high ball hitter. Equally, a low ball hitter's golf ball will be less influenced by a trailing wind. Obviously crosswinds will steer the ball in a sideways direction. Crosswinds can also affect the distance the golf ball travels. Imagine a right-handed golfer hitting a golf shot with a right to left wind. If the golfer hits the ball with a draw (right to left), the golf ball will tend to go its regular distance or a little further due to the ball moving on the wind for the last part of its journey. Conversely, if the golfer hits a fade (left to right), the ball will turn back into the wind, resulting in a reduction in distance. Working out the effect the wind has on your ball in terms of metres takes time. Keep a notepad in your golf bag to record how far your shots travel with each club in various wind conditions.

Of course, having a golf course well mapped out is only an advantage if you know how far you hit each club under still, normal conditions.

TERRAIN

Simply put, when you hit a golf ball uphill the ball will not go as far as when you hit it downhill. Like measuring the effect of wind, it takes time and experience to work out in terms of metres the effect an elevation change will have on your shots. As with wind, the height you hit your shots will determine how much influence the elevation change will have.

TEMPERATURE

The air temperature has a major effect on how far the ball flies because when it's warm the club compresses the ball far more than when it's cold. As the ball is compressed more, it creates more distance. In layman's terms, the golf ball will go further in the summer months than in the winter months. Like all other variables, it takes time and experience to learn the effect in terms of metres.

All these variables have an effect on the way you play. So often we see average golfers make strategic mistakes on the golf course, costing them countless shots. Can you picture a person walking onto a par 3 with a 5 iron in hand because the tee marker reads 150 metres. This player has taken none of the conditions mentioned above into account. However, the hole could

effectively be playing anywhere between 110 metres and 190 metres, depending on conditions. Keep your thinking cap on at all times. Always discuss conditions with your coach during a playing lesson.

PLAYING IT SMART

To score as low as you can on a consistent basis you must play to your strengths. Just because a golf hole is a par 4 or 5, it doesn't mean you should just pick the driver out of your bag and blindly blaze away. If you have mapped out your golf course properly, you should always know facts such as how far it is to the fairway bunkers, and how far to the dogleg and through the fairway from the tee, and so on.

As an example, if you typically drive the ball around 220 metres and there are fairway bunkers at 200 and 210 metres from the tee on a 350 metre par 4, hitting the driver is most probably a poor club selection. A 3 wood or even a 5 wood or long iron may be a far better choice. In this situation you really only require a tee shot of 180 to 200 metres, leaving you with 160 to 180 metres to the hole. You may think 'I don't want to be left with such a long second shot on a medium length par 4'. The reality is that your chances of avoiding the bunkers with the driver are nowhere near as good as hitting the fairway with the alternative club. As a result, the risk versus reward theory must be applied.

Remember, regardless of your choice of club from the tee, it is a two-shot golf hole. By that we mean that you can't reach the green from the tee, so is the reward of hitting a successful driver worth the risk? If instead of 220 metres, your average driving distance is 250 metres, hitting the driver would most probably be a wise play. This is because the fairway bunkers would not be in play, and hitting a 3 or 5 wood would only bring them into play.

It's not just bunkers that need to be avoided and negotiated. Water hazards, narrow portions of fairway with long rough, severe up or down slopes and out-of-bounds fences are examples of other obstacles you'll probably want to avoid.

Many golfers will fire at the flag, regardless of its location. This is a surefire way of never reaching your true potential. The best players in the world don't aim at every flag, so why should you? Playing to the centre of the green is far smarter for most golfers. Going for a flag that is cut tight near the edge of the green, and as a result missing that green on the side closest to the hole, is most commonly known as short-siding yourself. Getting the ball up and down from here is often all but impossible on most occasions.

Going for miracle or 'career' shots is another mistake many average golfers make. We have all found ourselves in the woods staring up through a gap in the trees barely large enough for the ball to fit through. It's a one in a 100 chance that many people take on. The result is usually catastrophic for your scorecard. The ball will most often ricochet further back into the woods into an even worse position. Had you chipped out onto the fairway, you may have salvaged a bogey instead of making an eight or nine on the hole.

The entire subject of course management is difficult to cover in one chapter of a book. There are just so many variables in golf courses and prevailing conditions. Having a playing lesson with your coach is paramount to understanding and improving your course management. The result will most definitely be better scores.

Mental focus

Following are a few ideas that will help you gain a greater control of your mind during play. Anyone wishing to delve into this subject in any depth may benefit from a consultation with a psychologist or reading one or more of a multitude of books specifically written on the subject. One thing is for sure. Anyone wishing to change the way they think on the golf course needs to have the desire within them to make the change. All the information in the world from psychologists and psychology books will not help unless you are genuinely prepared to work on techniques to help control your mental state.

Having control over your mind during a round of golf is, as every golfer knows, easier said than done. It's very easy to fall into the trap of riding golf's emotional roller–coaster, one minute thinking you are ready to take on the PGA Tour after consecutive birdies, the next minute contemplating giving up the game altogether after hitting consecutive tee shots out-of-bounds.

Golf can, without doubt, play severely with your emotions.

Owing to these emotional highs and lows, many poor strategic decisions are made, leading to poor scores. For example, a poor tee shot can often be a result of a three-putt green on the previous hole. The golfer, angry at the three putt, takes his or her frustration out on the tee shot on the next hole. It's not logical by any means, but many rational and intelligent people find themselves guilty of this type of behaviour.

STAYING IN THE PRESENT

Taking a 'stay-in-the-present' attitude towards the game is the most effective and simple way to keep off the emotional roller–coaster and limit anxiety.

Endeavouring to focus only on the shot at hand will help you to channel your energy into the present situation. Have you ever been playing a good round of golf and started to think of the upcoming holes? Standing on the 14th tee and realising your score is going along nicely, you begin to think things such as 'If I can just get through the next two holes I will be OK because 16 is an easy par and I always play 17 well and 18 is an easy par 5. What will I say in my speech when I win today's competition?' This is being mentally somewhere other than in the present. You are getting ahead of yourself. Just as lamenting over past actions can only be to your detriment, so too is looking into the future. After all, the only shot you can have any control over is the one you are about to hit. Any logical and rational person knows that you can't do anything about the past, and thinking about the future is pointless, so keep your mental state in the present. This type of attitude will help prevent unwanted anxiety.

Golfers who become overly anxious on the golf course are worried about the outcome. They are worried about events that have not yet happened. They are always thinking of something that could possibly go wrong. Staying focused on one shot at a time will assist in preventing the wasted emotion of anxiety.

A powerful example of what it might feel like to be 'in the zone' was Jack Nicklaus's answer to the question: 'What were you thinking down the final holes of your great wins, like the 1978 British Open at St Andrews and the 1986 US Masters?' He answered simply, 'nothing'. When challenged, he reiterated that 'I wanted nothing going through my mind'.*

* G. Crook – *The Golfer Magazine*, 19 November 1995.

A powerful example of what it might feel like to be 'in the zone' was Jack Nicklaus's answer to the question **'What were you thinking down the final holes of your great wins, like the 1978 British Open at St Andrews and the 1986 US Masters?'** He answered simply, **'nothing'**. When challenged, he reiterated that **'I wanted nothing going through my mind'.**

PRE-SHOT ROUTINE

A repetitive pre-shot routine is vital to establishing a sound and consistent golf game. Good visualisation skills are essential for success in any sport and golf is no exception. To be able to visualise a successful shot moments before you attempt to execute it facilitates a positive attitude which enhances your chances of success. This process should be included as an essential component of your pre-shot routine.

There are essentially only two parts to a pre-shot routine. The physical side and the mental side. The physical side of your routine consists of where you stand to begin your routine, and how many steps you take to get to the ball; how many practice swings and/or waggles you take; how you place your feet to make your stance; and how many looks you have at the target before you swing, and so on.

The mental side of your routine consists of your ability to visualise, your ability to keep your eyes only on the ball, the target line and the target, blocking out the bunkers, hazards and rough.

Successfully combining both the mental and physical components will create a repetitive routine that will help your golf game become more consistent, as well as aiding you in feeling more comfortable in pressure situations.

Your coach will assist you in building a pre-shot routine for your game – one that you are comfortable with; a routine that fits with your personality. It's not logical to build a routine consisting of three practice swings, multiple visualisations of the shot at hand, six steps to the ball, three waggles and three looks at the target if you are instinctively a quick player and the type of person who performs most daily activities in a fast manner. In other words, somebody who talks, walks and eats quickly should not have a long, slow and drawn-out routine. This kind of person requires a far more straight-to-the-point series of movements to get comfortable over the ball. The illustrations on pages 122–123 show just one example of a pre-shot routine. It should be noted that there are many other ways to approach it. You should discuss this with your coach.

In summary, it's crucial to acknowledge the importance of the mental side of golf. If you feel you require assistance in this area, talk to your golf coach. Most coaches have a working relationship with at least one sports psychologist.

Taking it to the course

OK. You understand the pitfalls that many people fall into when trying to improve their game and how to avoid them. You've selected a coach and made a commitment to have some consistent tuition. You've had a technical assessment, your coach knows what you're thinking, your equipment has been evaluated and you've committed to getting fit for golf. You have set a game plan in the form of a golf calendar and time wheel and broken your calendar up to cater for technical improvement time. And, of course, you've set your goals. Well done. You are now well on your way to enjoying the benefits of a better golf game.

It's now time to take it to the course. Part of your practice time has been spent hitting shots with a variety of clubs to various targets, not thinking about your technique. This is how you should play on the golf course. Because a large portion of your practice has been technically focused, you need to be able to let all those technical thoughts go and just focus on visualising the shot and then executing it without too much conscious thought.

Follow your golf time wheel and player's calendar religiously. Trust them. If your red zone has come to an end and it's time to enter the green zone, go ahead, even though you may not feel ready! The reality is that few are ever 100 per cent ready. It's time to go and play golf and enjoy it. Remember golf is a game for a lifetime and a never-ending journey. Technically, your golf swing will always be a 'work in progress'. See it this way and it will be easier to deal with your emotions.

We trust you now have a knowledge of some key fundamentals, how to approach having lessons and build a golf plan with your coach. Make your practice count and enjoy it.

The mental side of your routine consists of your ability to visualise, your ability to keep your eyes only on the ball, the target line and the target, blocking out the bunkers, hazards and rough.

Pre-shot routine

Decide exactly where to aim, what type of shot to play, and visualise that shot.

Visualise the shot with eyes closed.

Walk to the ball with the right hand on the grip of the club.

Align the club face with the right hand and the right foot forward.

Two hands on the club.

Put the feet into position, ready to swing.

I have enjoyed the experience of being involved in the making of **Playing your own golf game**. Being asked to be a model for the illustrations was certainly a big thrill for me. Rohan and Tim are true professionals; they made me feel welcome and worked tirelessly to put together what I believe is a truly wonderful teaching and coaching book. I hope that everyone who buys the book has as much fun and enjoyment reading and working through it as I did being involved in the making of it.

Jason Day – World Junior Golf Champion 2004
Australian Junior Champion 2004

7

Make your practice count

Golfer:

Coach:

Areas of your game

Technical

Playing

Golf plan

Mental

Physical

Coach's evaluation (✔ tick the standards)

Full swing   Date:

	GRIP	SET-UP	ALIGN	CLUB FACE	PIVOT	PLANE	RADIUS	IMPACT
EXCELLENT								
WORKABLE								
NEEDS WORK								
POOR								

COMMENTS

Coach's evaluation (✔ tick the standards)

Pitching   Date:

	GRIP	SET-UP	ALIGN	CLUB FACE	PIVOT	PLANE	RADIUS	IMPACT
EXCELLENT								
WORKABLE								
NEEDS WORK								
POOR								
COMMENTS								

Bunkers   Date:

	GRIP	SET-UP	ALIGN	CLUB FACE	PIVOT	PLANE	RADIUS	IMPACT
EXCELLENT								
WORKABLE								
NEEDS WORK								
POOR								
COMMENTS								

Coach's evaluation (✔ tick the standards)

Chipping   Date:

	GRIP	SET-UP	ALIGN	CLUB FACE	PIVOT	PLANE	RADIUS	IMPACT
EXCELLENT								
WORKABLE								
NEEDS WORK								
POOR								

COMMENTS

Putting   Date:

	GRIP	SET-UP	ALIGN	CLUB FACE	PIVOT	PLANE	RADIUS	IMPACT
EXCELLENT								
WORKABLE								
NEEDS WORK								
POOR								

COMMENTS

Re-evaluation (✔ tick the standards)

Full swing					Date:			
	GRIP	SET-UP	ALIGN	CLUB FACE	PIVOT	PLANE	RADIUS	IMPACT
EXCELLENT								
WORKABLE								
NEEDS WORK								
POOR								

COMMENTS

Re-evaluation (✔ tick the standards)

Pitching   Date:

	GRIP	SET-UP	ALIGN	CLUB FACE	PIVOT	PLANE	RADIUS	IMPACT
EXCELLENT								
WORKABLE								
NEEDS WORK								
POOR								

COMMENTS

Bunkers   Date:

	GRIP	SET-UP	ALIGN	CLUB FACE	PIVOT	PLANE	RADIUS	IMPACT
EXCELLENT								
WORKABLE								
NEEDS WORK								
POOR								

COMMENTS

Re-evaluation (✔ tick the standards)

Chipping — Date:

	GRIP	SET-UP	ALIGN	CLUB FACE	PIVOT	PLANE	RADIUS	IMPACT
EXCELLENT								
WORKABLE								
NEEDS WORK								
POOR								

COMMENTS

Putting — Date:

	GRIP	SET-UP	ALIGN	CLUB FACE	PIVOT	PLANE	RADIUS	IMPACT
EXCELLENT								
WORKABLE								
NEEDS WORK								
POOR								

COMMENTS

Club evaluation chart – Do your clubs suit you?

SPECIFICATIONS OF YOUR CURRENT CLUBS	SPECIFICATIONS	COACH'S COMMENTS	DATE
IRONS			
Length – i.e. – STD +1" etc.			
Lie angle of head			
Shaft flex			
Shaft deflection point			
Shaft type – i.e. graphite – steel			
Grip thickness			
Set configuration i.e. 2 – Lob wedge			
WOODS			
Length of driver			
Length of fairway woods			
Driver loft			
Shaft flex			
Shaft deflection point			
Shaft type – i.e. graphite – steel			
Grip thickness			
Wood configuration i.e. 1–3–5			

Club fitting chart

Date	**Order date**
Fitting professional	
Customer name	
Address	
Telephone	**Work**
Home	
Mobile	**Email**
Woods maufacturer	**Model**
Irons manufacturer	**Model**
Right hand ☐ **Left hand** ☐	**Lie angle**
Shaft type	**Shaft flex**
Woods set make up 1 3 5 7 9 11	**Driver loft**
Iron set make up 2 3 4 5 6 7 8 9 PW GAP SW LW	
	Total
Order **Woods @ $**	
Order **Irons @ $**	
Order **Putters @ $**	
Order **Bags @ $**	
Order **Miscellaneous @ $**	
	Total cost $
	Deposit $
	Balance
	Receipt number

Putter face alignment

Test (✔) to be repeated 5 times on each date.

DATE	ALIGNMENT OUTSIDE LEFT EDGE	ALIGNMENT LEFT EDGE	ALIGNMENT STRAIGHT	ALIGNMENT RIGHT EDGE	ALIGNMENT OUTSIDE RIGHT EDGE

Putter face alignment

Test (✔) to be repeated 5 times on each date.

DATE	ALIGNMENT OUTSIDE LEFT EDGE	ALIGNMENT LEFT EDGE	ALIGNMENT STRAIGHT	ALIGNMENT RIGHT EDGE	ALIGNMENT OUTSIDE RIGHT EDGE

Questionnaire of beliefs

After listing your beliefs below, you need to answer the questions that follow, giving a yes or no, providing a key reason for your answer. Present this to your coach for discussion. Take your time answering these questions and make as many written comments with your yes/no answers as you wish. Your coach will be very interested in your answers.

What are you thinking?

- List any beliefs you have regarding golf technique.

What are you thinking?

(circle and comment)

• At the address position with the full swing,
should your head be in line with the golf ball?

YES / NO

• At the address position with the full swing,
should your shoulders be level?

YES / NO

• Should you keep your head down at the address position?

YES / NO

• Should your grip pressure be reasonably
firm during the full swing?

YES / NO

What are you thinking?

(circle and comment)

- With any shot, such as the full swing, pitching, chipping, bunkers and putting, should the club head be drawn away from the ball in a perfectly straight line, directly away from the intended target for at least a metre? (If so, which shots?) **YES / NO**

- With any shot, should the club face stay pointing towards the target in the takeaway? (If so, which shots?) **YES / NO**

- With the full swing, should the leading arm stay rigid in the backswing? **YES / NO**

- With the full swing, should the trailing arm tuck into your trailing side during the backswing? **YES / NO**

- With the full swing, should your head stay perfectly still until after impact? **YES / NO**

What are you thinking?

(circle and comment)

• With the full swing, in the backswing should you move your hips laterally to transfer weight to the trailing leg?

YES / NO

• With the full swing at impact, should your club head be on its way up to help the ball become airborne?

YES / NO

• With the full swing, should the impact position of the body and the club shaft be the same as the address position?

YES / NO

• With the full swing after impact, should you keep your head down?

YES / NO

• With the full swing after impact, should the direction of the club head go straight towards the intended target?

YES / NO

On-course self-assessment   Course   Date

Before your round of golf, did you:	**CIRCLE YOUR ANSWER**
• warm up (i.e. exercise/stretch)?	**YES / NO**
• hit 30 range balls or more?	**YES / NO**
• have 30 practice swings or more?	**YES / NO**
• have a practice putt for ten minutes or more?	**YES / NO**

From tee to green, did you:	
• genuinely visualise every shot before you hit it?	**YES / NO**
• mentally stay in the present and think of only one shot at a time?	**YES / NO**
• maintain a consistent pre-shot routine throughout the entire round?	**YES / NO**
• have a maximum of two swing thoughts for the entire round?	**YES / NO**
• aim away from the flagstick when required?	**YES / NO**
• take conditions such as wind and terrain into account with every golf shot?	**YES / NO**

On the greens did you:	
• get 90% or more of your makeable putts to the hole?	**YES / NO**
• miss 90% of your makeable putts on the high side of the hole?	**YES / NO**

If you didn't answer yes to at least 9 of these 12 questions, your preparation and course management requires work.

Re-assessment   Course   Date

Before your round of golf, did you: CIRCLE YOUR ANSWER

- warm up (i.e. exercise/stretch)?   YES / NO
- hit 30 range balls or more?   YES / NO
- have 30 practice swings or more?   YES / NO
- have a practice putt for ten minutes or more?   YES / NO

From tee to green, did you:

- genuinely visualise every shot before you hit it?   YES / NO
- mentally stay in the present and think of
  only one shot at a time?   YES / NO
- maintain a consistent pre-shot routine throughout
  the entire round?   YES / NO
- have a maximum of two swing thoughts for the entire round?   YES / NO
- aim away from the flagstick when required?   YES / NO
- take conditions such as wind and terrain into account
  with every golf shot?   YES / NO

On the greens did you:

- get 90% or more of your makeable putts to the hole?   YES / NO
- miss 90% of your makeable putts on the high
  side of the hole?   YES / NO

If you didn't answer yes to at least 9 of these 12 questions,
your preparation and course management requires work.

Self-test 1 Extension drill – Angel wings against wall

Stand with your back against a wall. Pull your shoulder blades back and down towards your tailbone, tuck your chin in as though you are making a double chin, and suck your belly button in towards your spine. Place the backs of your arms, the backs of your hands and thumbs against the wall. Keep your feet together, pointing directly forwards, with the backs of your heels against the wall with your shoes on.

CHECK (CIRCLE ANSWER)	DATE	DATE
Shoulders against wall	YES / NO	YES / NO
Wrists against wall	YES / NO	YES / NO
Middle of back against wall	YES / NO	YES / NO
Skull against wall	YES / NO	YES / NO

DISCLAIMER It is advisable that you consult a physiotherapist or doctor before performing any of the following tests to ensure there is no medical reason why you shouldn't engage in this type of activity.

Self-test 2 Rotation drill – Spinal rotation in standing position, using golf club

Standing with your feet approximately shoulder width apart, place a club in the crook of both arms behind your back, about halfway up your spine. Keeping your shoulders level and preventing your hips from any sideways movement, slowly rotate the club to the right and then to the left. Take a visual measurement of how far the club travels in each direction.

CHECK (CIRCLE ANSWER)	DATE	DATE
Club stays on back up to 90 degrees rotation	YES / NO	YES / NO
Hips stay straight and level facing forward	YES / NO	YES / NO
Shoulders stay back and down	YES / NO	YES / NO

Self-test 3 Flexibility drill – Trunk drill on one knee

Kneeling on one knee, lunge forward until you first feel a pulling sensation at the front of the hip on the side which has the knee on the ground. Make sure your front knee and foot are pointing directly forward. Then, holding the club above your head, bend to the side away from the knee on the ground. Be sure to keep your shoulders straight and your chest facing directly forward.

CHECK (CIRCLE ANSWER)	DATE	DATE
Upper body stays straight, facing forward	YES / NO	YES / NO
Knee stays straight	YES / NO	YES / NO
Hips stay straight	YES / NO	YES / NO
Neck and shoulders stay in alignment with the rest of the body	YES / NO	YES / NO

Self-test 4 Core stability drill – Dead bug using posture bar or 30 cm ruler

Lying on your back with your hips and knees bent to 90 degrees, hold the posture bar between your ankles. Keep the back of your hands, arms, and back flat on the floor allowing for the natural curve of the lower back. Don't let your knees fall towards each other.

CHECK (CIRCLE ANSWER)	DATE	DATE
Middle and upper back stays on the ground	YES / NO	YES / NO
Both knees stay even	YES / NO	YES / NO
Feel activation below belly button	YES / NO	YES / NO
Feel activation in inner thighs	YES / NO	YES / NO

Self-test 5 Balance drill – Bar lifts with posture bar or 30 cm ruler

Using a wall for support, place the posture bar between the insides of your feet (on the bones just below the big toes). Place your arms by your side and the back of your hands against the wall. Slowly lift the bar up off the ground with your feet, maintaining good posture at all times.

CHECK (CIRCLE ANSWER)	DATE	DATE
Shoulders stay back and down	YES / NO	YES / NO
Lower back stays flat	YES / NO	YES / NO
Feel activation below belly button	YES / NO	YES / NO
Feel activation in inner thighs	YES / NO	YES / NO

Self-test physical summary

Having performed the five self-test drills, it's now time to evaluate your body's suitability for golf.

If you answered yes to **15 to 18 questions**, your physiological condition is more than likely quite good. Although your body will probably be capable of swinging a golf club effectively, you may still not be capable of maintaining correct positions and posture over 18 holes of golf or during a practice session. Performing these drills on a regular basis will enable your form and posture to be sustainable for a longer period.

If you answered yes to **12 to 14 questions**, it means your form is breaking down and you are struggling to maintain correct position and posture. The same thing will almost certainly occur during your golf swing, rendering you incapable of swinging a golf club in a technically correct manner.

If you answered yes to **11 or less questions,** it means that your body is not suitable for playing good golf. You are likely to have a problem with strength and flexibility, as your body is not sequencing properly. You will be highly susceptible to back, neck and shoulder injuries. Consulting a qualified physiotherapist is advisable.

Postural screening summary

Mark the boxes ✔ = yes ✘ = no (to be completed by physiotherapist)

POSTURE TEST
Good posture = Posture for golf

WALL POSTURE ❑
Keeping your knees and trunk against the wall and your arms at 90 degrees and wrists flat to the wall.

FLEXIBILITY TEST
To check your range throughout the golf swing. These muscles listed right usually get tight through sitting at a computer or in a car. They can also get over-tight with poor practice regimes.

AREA	RIGHT	LEFT
Pectorals	❑	❑
Biceps	❑	❑
Trapezius	❑	❑
Levator scapulae	❑	❑
Quadratus lumborum	❑	❑
Hip flexors	❑	❑
Hamstrings	❑	❑
Gluteals	❑	❑
Calves	❑	❑

ROTATION TEST
To ensure you rotate correctly in your golf swing rather than compensate with your arms, hands and feet.

SPINAL LOCATION
Cervical spine	❑	❑
Thoracic spine	❑	❑
Lumbar spine	❑	❑

Comments

Postural screening summary

Mark the boxes ✔ = yes ✘ = no (to be completed by physiotherapist)

EXTENSION TEST

To ensure that you maintain good upright
and athletic posture at address.

DOORWAY DRILL ❏

Stand in between the doorway with your
elbows at right angles and lean forward
letting your forearms support you. Keeping
your neck in a neutral position with your ear
in line with your shoulder, and making sure
your tummy is kept sucked in without your
pelvis tilting forward and your back arching.

CORE STABILITY TEST

To ensure you sequence and use the large
golf muscles correctly in your golf swing.

SWISS BALL TEST ❏

Test or biofeedback ❏

BALANCE / FEEL TEST

To ensure good weight transference
and balance within your golf swing.

WOBBLE BOARD TEST ❏

Eyes shut ❏

Comments

Goal setting

DATE:

OUTCOME GOALS:

PROCESS GOALS:

Goal setting

DATE:

OUTCOME GOALS:

PROCESS GOALS:

Goal setting

DATE:

OUTCOME GOALS:

PROCESS GOALS:

Player's calendar

First calendar

Jan	Feb	Mar	April	May	June	Jul	Aug	Sept	Oct	Nov	Dec

Second calendar

Jan	Feb	Mar	April	May	June	Jul	Aug	Sept	Oct	Nov	Dec

Third calendar

Jan	Feb	Mar	April	May	June	Jul	Aug	Sept	Oct	Nov	Dec

Fourth calendar

Jan	Feb	Mar	April	May	June	Jul	Aug	Sept	Oct	Nov	Dec

Golf time wheel

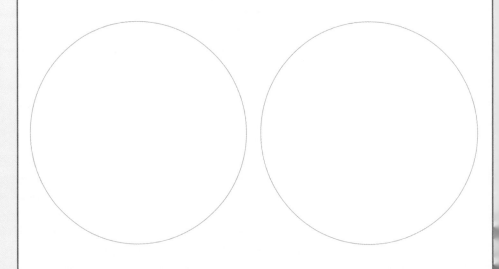

YOUR INITIAL TIME WHEEL   **DATE**

The first **golf time wheel** is to be filled out by your coach as soon as you have completed your full assessment. We recommend that your coach reassesses your practice program periodically and, therefore, fills out a new time wheel whenever a change in program is required.

RED ZONE   **GREEN ZONE**

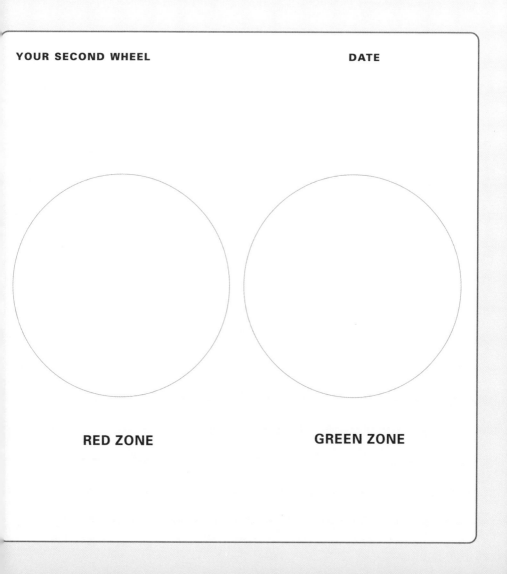

YOUR SECOND WHEEL

DATE

RED ZONE

GREEN ZONE

Golf time wheel (cont'd)

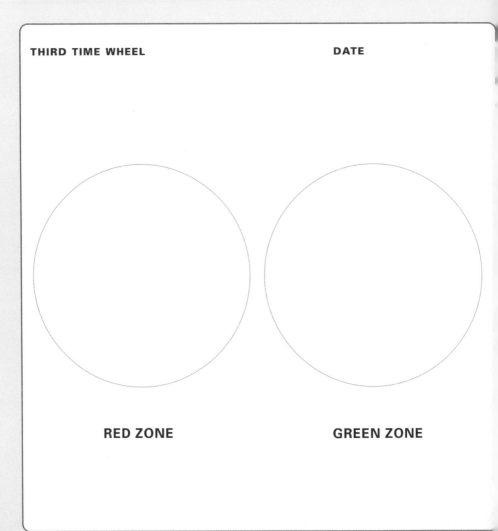

THIRD TIME WHEEL   DATE

RED ZONE   **GREEN ZONE**

FOURTH TIME WHEEL

DATE

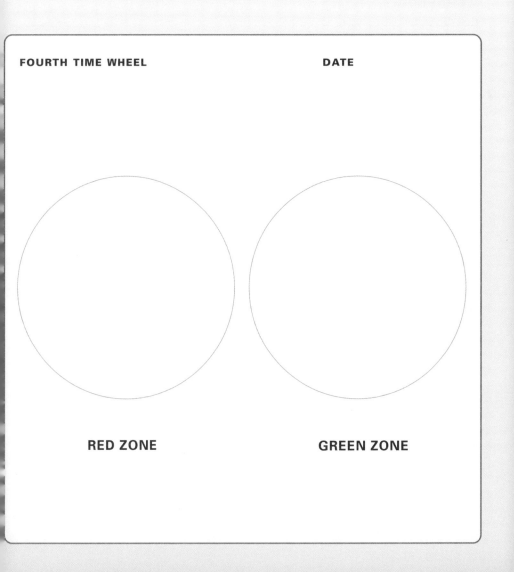

RED ZONE

GREEN ZONE

Lesson note

DATE:	(Circle area you are working on)

GRIP	SET-UP	ALIGNMENT	PIVOT	PLANE	RELEASE	PITCHING
CHIPPING	BUNKER	PUTTING	NON–TECH PRACTICE	COURSE MGT	MENTAL MGT	

COACH CONCERNS

SUGGESTED CHANGES

DRILLS TO PRACTISE

PLAYER'S REACTION

Lesson note

DATE:	(Circle area you are working on)

GRIP   SET-UP   ALIGNMENT   PIVOT   PLANE   RELEASE   PITCHING
CHIPPING   BUNKER   PUTTING   NON–TECH PRACTICE   COURSE MGT   MENTAL MGT

COACH CONCERNS

SUGGESTED CHANGES

DRILLS TO PRACTISE

PLAYER'S REACTION

Lesson note

DATE: (Circle area you are working on)

| GRIP | SET-UP | ALIGNMENT | PIVOT | PLANE | RELEASE | PITCHING |
| CHIPPING | BUNKER | PUTTING | NON–TECH | PRACTICE | COURSE MGT | MENTAL MGT |

COACH CONCERNS

SUGGESTED CHANGES

DRILLS TO PRACTISE

PLAYER'S REACTION

Lesson note

DATE:	(Circle area you are working on)

GRIP	SET-UP	ALIGNMENT	PIVOT	PLANE	RELEASE	PITCHING
CHIPPING	BUNKER	PUTTING	NON–TECH PRACTICE	COURSE MGT	MENTAL MGT	

COACH CONCERNS

SUGGESTED CHANGES

DRILLS TO PRACTISE

PLAYER'S REACTION

Lesson note

DATE:	(Circle area you are working on)

GRIP	SET-UP	ALIGNMENT	PIVOT	PLANE	RELEASE	PITCHING
CHIPPING	BUNKER	PUTTING	NON–TECH	PRACTICE	COURSE MGT	MENTAL MGT

COACH CONCERNS

SUGGESTED CHANGES

DRILLS TO PRACTISE

PLAYER'S REACTION

Lesson note

DATE:					(Circle area you are working on)	
GRIP	SET-UP	ALIGNMENT	PIVOT	PLANE	RELEASE	PITCHING
CHIPPING	BUNKER	PUTTING	NON–TECH PRACTICE		COURSE MGT	MENTAL MGT

COACH CONCERNS

SUGGESTED CHANGES

DRILLS TO PRACTISE

PLAYER'S REACTION

Lesson note

DATE:					(Circle area you are working on)

GRIP   SET-UP   ALIGNMENT   PIVOT   PLANE   RELEASE   PITCHING

CHIPPING   BUNKER   PUTTING   NON–TECH PRACTICE   COURSE MGT   MENTAL MGT

COACH CONCERNS

SUGGESTED CHANGES

DRILLS TO PRACTISE

PLAYER'S REACTION

Lesson note

DATE: (Circle area you are working on)

GRIP   SET-UP   ALIGNMENT   PIVOT   PLANE   RELEASE   PITCHING
CHIPPING   BUNKER   PUTTING   NON–TECH PRACTICE   COURSE MGT   MENTAL MGT

COACH CONCERNS

SUGGESTED CHANGES

DRILLS TO PRACTISE

PLAYER'S REACTION

Lesson note

| DATE: | | | | | | (Circle area you are working on) |

| GRIP | SET-UP | ALIGNMENT | PIVOT | PLANE | RELEASE | PITCHING |
| CHIPPING | BUNKER | PUTTING | NON–TECH | PRACTICE | COURSE MGT | MENTAL MGT |

COACH CONCERNS

SUGGESTED CHANGES

DRILLS TO PRACTISE

PLAYER'S REACTION

Lesson note

DATE:					(Circle area you are working on)	
GRIP	SET-UP	ALIGNMENT	PIVOT	PLANE	RELEASE	PITCHING
CHIPPING	BUNKER	PUTTING	NON–TECH PRACTICE		COURSE MGT	MENTAL MGT

COACH CONCERNS

SUGGESTED CHANGES

DRILLS TO PRACTISE

PLAYER'S REACTION

Lesson note

DATE:	(Circle area you are working on)

GRIP   SET-UP   ALIGNMENT   PIVOT   PLANE   RELEASE   PITCHING
CHIPPING   BUNKER   PUTTING   NON–TECH PRACTICE   COURSE MGT   MENTAL MGT

COACH CONCERNS

SUGGESTED CHANGES

DRILLS TO PRACTISE

PLAYER'S REACTION

Lesson note

DATE:	(Circle area you are working on)

| GRIP | SET-UP | ALIGNMENT | PIVOT | PLANE | RELEASE | PITCHING |
| CHIPPING | BUNKER | PUTTING | NON–TECH PRACTICE | COURSE MGT | MENTAL MGT |

COACH CONCERNS

SUGGESTED CHANGES

DRILLS TO PRACTISE

PLAYER'S REACTION

Lesson note

| DATE: | (Circle area you are working on) |

| GRIP | SET-UP | ALIGNMENT | PIVOT | PLANE | RELEASE | PITCHING |
| CHIPPING | BUNKER | PUTTING | NON–TECH PRACTICE | COURSE MGT | MENTAL MGT |

COACH CONCERNS

SUGGESTED CHANGES

DRILLS TO PRACTISE

PLAYER'S REACTION

Lesson note

DATE:	(Circle area you are working on)

| GRIP | SET-UP | ALIGNMENT | PIVOT | PLANE | RELEASE | PITCHING |
| CHIPPING | BUNKER | PUTTING | NON–TECH | PRACTICE | COURSE MGT | MENTAL MGT |

COACH CONCERNS

SUGGESTED CHANGES

DRILLS TO PRACTISE

PLAYER'S REACTION

Lesson note

DATE: (Circle area you are working on)

GRIP   SET-UP   ALIGNMENT   PIVOT   PLANE   RELEASE   PITCHING

CHIPPING   BUNKER   PUTTING   NON–TECH PRACTICE   COURSE MGT   MENTAL MGT

COACH CONCERNS

SUGGESTED CHANGES

DRILLS TO PRACTISE

PLAYER'S REACTION

Lesson note

DATE: (Circle area you are working on)

GRIP   SET-UP   ALIGNMENT   PIVOT   PLANE   RELEASE   PITCHING
CHIPPING   BUNKER   PUTTING   NON–TECH PRACTICE   COURSE MGT   MENTAL MGT

COACH CONCERNS

SUGGESTED CHANGES

DRILLS TO PRACTISE

PLAYER'S REACTION

Lesson note

DATE:	(Circle area you are working on)

GRIP	SET-UP	ALIGNMENT	PIVOT	PLANE	RELEASE	PITCHING
CHIPPING	BUNKER	PUTTING	NON–TECH	PRACTICE	COURSE MGT	MENTAL MGT

COACH CONCERNS

SUGGESTED CHANGES

DRILLS TO PRACTISE

PLAYER'S REACTION

Lesson note

DATE:	(Circle area you are working on)

GRIP   SET-UP   ALIGNMENT   PIVOT   PLANE   RELEASE   PITCHING
CHIPPING   BUNKER   PUTTING   NON–TECH PRACTICE   COURSE MGT   MENTAL MGT

COACH CONCERNS

SUGGESTED CHANGES

DRILLS TO PRACTISE

PLAYER'S REACTION

Lesson note

DATE: (Circle area you are working on)

| GRIP | SET-UP | ALIGNMENT | PIVOT | PLANE | RELEASE | PITCHING |
| CHIPPING | BUNKER | PUTTING | NON–TECH | PRACTICE | COURSE MGT | MENTAL MGT |

COACH CONCERNS

SUGGESTED CHANGES

DRILLS TO PRACTISE

PLAYER'S REACTION

Lesson note

DATE:	(Circle area you are working on)

GRIP   SET-UP   ALIGNMENT   PIVOT   PLANE   RELEASE   PITCHING

CHIPPING   BUNKER   PUTTING   NON–TECH   PRACTICE   COURSE MGT   MENTAL MGT

COACH CONCERNS

SUGGESTED CHANGES

DRILLS TO PRACTISE

PLAYER'S REACTION

Round summary   Golf course: Date:

	PAR	FAIRWAYS	GREENS	PITCHING	CHIPPING	BUNKERS	PUTTS	SCORE
1		Y N	Y N					
2		Y N	Y N					
3		Y N	Y N					
4		Y N	Y N					
5		Y N	Y N					
6		Y N	Y N					
7		Y N	Y N					
8		Y N	Y N					
9		Y N	Y N					
10		Y N	Y N					
11		Y N	Y N					
12		Y N	Y N					
13		Y N	Y N					
14		Y N	Y N					
15		Y N	Y N					
16		Y N	Y N					
17		Y N	Y N					
18		Y N	Y N					
Total								

Comment:

Round summary   Golf course: Date:

	PAR	FAIRWAYS	GREENS	PITCHING		CHIPPING		BUNKERS	PUTTS	SCORE
1		Y N	Y N							
2		Y N	Y N							
3		Y N	Y N							
4		Y N	Y N							
5		Y N	Y N							
6		Y N	Y N							
7		Y N	Y N							
8		Y N	Y N							
9		Y N	Y N							
10		Y N	Y N							
11		Y N	Y N							
12		Y N	Y N							
13		Y N	Y N							
14		Y N	Y N							
15		Y N	Y N							
16		Y N	Y N							
17		Y N	Y N							
18		Y N	Y N							
Total										
Comment:										

Round summary   Golf course: Date:

	PAR	FAIRWAYS	GREENS	PITCHING	CHIPPING	BUNKERS	PUTTS	SCORE
1		Y N	Y N					
2		Y N	Y N					
3		Y N	Y N					
4		Y N	Y N					
5		Y N	Y N					
6		Y N	Y N					
7		Y N	Y N					
8		Y N	Y N					
9		Y N	Y N					
10		Y N	Y N					
11		Y N	Y N					
12		Y N	Y N					
13		Y N	Y N					
14		Y N	Y N					
15		Y N	Y N					
16		Y N	Y N					
17		Y N	Y N					
18		Y N	Y N					
Total								

Comment:

Round summary   Golf course: Date:

	PAR	FAIRWAYS	GREENS	PITCHING	CHIPPING	BUNKERS	PUTTS	SCORE
1		Y N	Y N					
2		Y N	Y N					
3		Y N	Y N					
4		Y N	Y N					
5		Y N	Y N					
6		Y N	Y N					
7		Y N	Y N					
8		Y N	Y N					
9		Y N	Y N					
10		Y N	Y N					
11		Y N	Y N					
12		Y N	Y N					
13		Y N	Y N					
14		Y N	Y N					
15		Y N	Y N					
16		Y N	Y N					
17		Y N	Y N					
18		Y N	Y N					
Total								

Comment:

Round summary   Golf course: Date:

	PAR	FAIRWAYS	GREENS	PITCHING	CHIPPING	BUNKERS	PUTTS	SCORE
1		Y N	Y N					
2		Y N	Y N					
3		Y N	Y N					
4		Y N	Y N					
5		Y N	Y N					
6		Y N	Y N					
7		Y N	Y N					
8		Y N	Y N					
9		Y N	Y N					
10		Y N	Y N					
11		Y N	Y N					
12		Y N	Y N					
13		Y N	Y N					
14		Y N	Y N					
15		Y N	Y N					
16		Y N	Y N					
17		Y N	Y N					
18		Y N	Y N					
Total								
Comment:								

Round summary

Golf course: Date:

	PAR	FAIRWAYS	GREENS	PITCHING	CHIPPING	BUNKERS	PUTTS	SCORE
1		Y N	Y N					
2		Y N	Y N					
3		Y N	Y N					
4		Y N	Y N					
5		Y N	Y N					
6		Y N	Y N					
7		Y N	Y N					
8		Y N	Y N					
9		Y N	Y N					
10		Y N	Y N					
11		Y N	Y N					
12		Y N	Y N					
13		Y N	Y N					
14		Y N	Y N					
15		Y N	Y N					
16		Y N	Y N					
17		Y N	Y N					
18		Y N	Y N					
Total								

Comment:

Round summary   Golf course: Date:

	PAR	FAIRWAYS	GREENS	PITCHING	CHIPPING	BUNKERS	PUTTS	SCORE
1		Y N	Y N					
2		Y N	Y N					
3		Y N	Y N					
4		Y N	Y N					
5		Y N	Y N					
6		Y N	Y N					
7		Y N	Y N					
8		Y N	Y N					
9		Y N	Y N					
10		Y N	Y N					
11		Y N	Y N					
12		Y N	Y N					
13		Y N	Y N					
14		Y N	Y N					
15		Y N	Y N					
16		Y N	Y N					
17		Y N	Y N					
18		Y N	Y N					
Total								

Comment:

Round summary   Golf course: Date:

	PAR	FAIRWAYS	GREENS	PITCHING	CHIPPING	BUNKERS	PUTTS	SCORE
1		Y N	Y N					
2		Y N	Y N					
3		Y N	Y N					
4		Y N	Y N					
5		Y N	Y N					
6		Y N	Y N					
7		Y N	Y N					
8		Y N	Y N					
9		Y N	Y N					
10		Y N	Y N					
11		Y N	Y N					
12		Y N	Y N					
13		Y N	Y N					
14		Y N	Y N					
15		Y N	Y N					
16		Y N	Y N					
17		Y N	Y N					
18		Y N	Y N					
Total								

Comment:

Round summary   Golf course: Date:

	PAR	FAIRWAYS	GREENS	PITCHING	CHIPPING	BUNKERS	PUTTS	SCORE
1		Y N	Y N					
2		Y N	Y N					
3		Y N	Y N					
4		Y N	Y N					
5		Y N	Y N					
6		Y N	Y N					
7		Y N	Y N					
8		Y N	Y N					
9		Y N	Y N					
10		Y N	Y N					
11		Y N	Y N					
12		Y N	Y N					
13		Y N	Y N					
14		Y N	Y N					
15		Y N	Y N					
16		Y N	Y N					
17		Y N	Y N					
18		Y N	Y N					
Total								

Comment:

Round summary   Golf course: Date:

	PAR	FAIRWAYS	GREENS	PITCHING		CHIPPING		BUNKERS		PUTTS	SCORE
1		Y N	Y N								
2		Y N	Y N								
3		Y N	Y N								
4		Y N	Y N								
5		Y N	Y N								
6		Y N	Y N								
7		Y N	Y N								
8		Y N	Y N								
9		Y N	Y N								
10		Y N	Y N								
11		Y N	Y N								
12		Y N	Y N								
13		Y N	Y N								
14		Y N	Y N								
15		Y N	Y N								
16		Y N	Y N								
17		Y N	Y N								
18		Y N	Y N								
Total											

Comment:

Ten round summary – Statistic records

DATE	GOLF COURSE	PAR	FAIRWAY REG	GREEN REG	PITCHING UP/DOWN		CHIP UP/DOWN		BUNKER UP/DOWN		TOTAL PUTTS	SCORE
10/8/04	RM–West	72	8	8	1	1	3	1	3	1	31	79

DATE	GOLF COURSE	PAR	FAIRWAY REG	GREEN REG	PITCHING UP/DOWN		CHIP UP/DOWN		BUNKER UP/DOWN		TOTAL PUTTS	SCORE
		PAR	FAIRWAY REG	GREEN REG	PITCHING UP/DOWN		CHIP UP/DOWN		BUNKER UP/DOWN		TOTAL PUTTS	SCORE
TOTAL												
TOTAL AVERAGES												